Assessing Middle and High School Mathematics and Science

Differentiating Formative Assessment

Sheryn Spencer Waterman

EYE ON EDUCATION
6 DEPOT WAY WEST, SUITE 106
LARCHMONT, NY 10538
(914) 833–0551
(914) 833–0761 fax
www.eyeoneducation.com

Library of Congress Cataloging-in-Publication Data

Waterman, Sheryn Spencer.

  Assessing middle and high school mathematics and science : differentiating formative assessment / Sheryn Spencer Waterman.

    p. cm.

  ISBN 978-1-59667-149-2

  1. Mathematics--Study and teaching (Middle school) 2. Mathematics--Study and teaching (Secondary) 3. Science--Study and teaching (Middle school) 4. Science--Study and teaching (Secondary) 5. Mathematical readiness. 6. Individualized instruction. I. Title.

  QA11.2.W374 2010

  507.1'2--dc22

                                                                        2010004548

10 9 8 7 6 5 4 3 2 1

Also Available from EYE ON EDUCATION

**Differentiating Assessment in Middle and High
School Mathematics and Science**
Sheryn Spencer Waterman

**Assessing Middle and High School Social Studies and
English: Differentiating Formative Assessment**
Sheryn Spencer Waterman

**Differentiating Assessment in Middle and High
School English and Social Studies**
Sheryn Spencer Waterman

Handbook on Differentiated Instruction for Middle and High Schools
Sheryn Spencer Northey

**Teaching, Learning, and Assessment Together: Reflective
Assessments for Middle & High School Mathematics & Science**
Arthur Ellis and David Denton

Differentiated Assessment for Middle and High School Classrooms
Deborah Blaz

**Teacher-Made Assessments: Connecting Curriculum,
Instruction, and Student Learning**
Christopher R. Gareis and Leslie W. Grant

**Critical Thinking and Formative Assessments:
Increasing the Rigor in Your Classroom**
Betsy Moore and Todd Stanley

**Assessment in Middle and High School Mathematics:
A Teacher's Guide**
Daniel Brahier

**A Collection of Performance Tasks and Rubrics:
Primary School Mathematics**
Charlotte Danielson and Pia Hansen Powell

Upper Elementary School Mathematics
Charlotte Danielson

Middle School Mathematics
Charlotte Danielson

High School Mathematics
Charlotte Danielson and Elizabeth Marquez

Disclaimer

Some of the strategies explained in this book are from a collection of ideas I have gathered as a teacher. I have made every effort to determine their sources; however, if the originators of any of them feel they need to be cited, please contact me. Send an e-mail to author@eyeoneducation.com and type my name in the subject line.

— Sheryn Spencer Waterman

Meet the Author

Sheryn Spencer Waterman is an educational consultant and instructional coach who specializes in curriculum design, differentiation, assessment, literacy, and mentoring. Her many accomplishments include "Teacher of the Year" in two schools, National Board Certification (renewed 2007), and Founding Fellow for the Teacher's Network Leadership Institute. She came to the field of education after a career as a psychotherapist and consultant. She has contributed to many local, state, regional, and national projects to promote quality teaching, and she is working on a doctorate in teacher education at the University of North Carolina at Greensboro.

Free Downloads

Selected figures in this book can be downloaded and printed out by anyone who has purchased this book. Book buyers have permission to download and print out these Adobe Acrobat documents.

You can access these downloads by visiting Eye On Education's website: www. eyeoneducation.com. Click on "Free Downloads," or find this book on our website and then scroll down for downloading instructions.

You'll need your book-buyer access code: **DFMS-7153-9**

Contents

Preface

This book is for teachers and administrators who are committed to helping *all* of their students learn mathematics and science concepts and facts. In the first chapter, readers will find ideas that convert differentiation and assessment theory to practice. For example, I answer questions like "What is differentiation?," "Why differentiate assessment?," and "What is formative assessment? I include ideas that teachers can apply generally to plan differentiated formative assessment schedules and how they might collaborate with others to improve assessment processes. Each chapter that follows provides detailed examples of how teachers might apply curriculum standards reflected in essential questions that help them to as clearly as possible determine what they want their students to know, understand, and do as a result of the classroom experience. The examples also suggest ideas for developing measurable objectives that teachers differentiate by readiness (three levels), interests, and learning styles. I chose to provide examples based on the psychological theories of Carl Jung (1923) and adjusted for the classroom teacher by Silver, Strong, and Perini (2007). I think these ideas provide one of the most useful models for differentiating formative assessment in middle and high school classrooms. Teachers will find step-by-step procedures that should inspire them to create their own lessons. I indicate places in the procedures where teachers might use a differentiated formative assessment (DFA) to determine whether they want to adjust their instruction for the whole class, for small groups, or for individuals. Meeting the needs of *all* students in middle and high school is a tremendous challenge, but if you chose this book, you acknowledge that you are willing to meet that challenge.

1

Differentiating Formative Assessment

What is Differentiation?

Differentiation is the process of tailoring instruction to meet the needs of *all* students. Teachers who choose to practice differentiated instruction (DI) do the following:

- Learn about their students in terms of the following: their readiness to learn content, their interests in conjunction with that content, and their learning or thinking styles that might allow them greater access to that content;

- Gather content resources that match students' readiness, interests, and learning styles;

- Choose a process, such as flexible grouping, individualized instruction, or lesson tiering to address students' readiness, interests, and learning styles; and

- Plan assessments that address students' readiness, interests, and learning styles.

This book focuses on embedding formative assessment within a procedure that addresses the overall process of differentiating instruction, including providing suggestions for three levels of readiness: struggling learners, typical learners, and gifted or highly advanced learners.*

Why Differentiate Assessment?

Differentiating assessment is the only *fair* way to evaluate students' learning. According to Rick Wormeli (2006), "What is fair isn't always equal, and our goal as teachers is to be fair and developmentally appropriate, not one-size-fits all equal" (p. 6). If we give every child the same assessment, we are not paying attention to students' different learning styles and academic readiness. This book is based on the idea that teachers make a curriculum plan that *aims* different kinds of learners toward a *target* learning focus. Then as the lesson proceeds, these teachers constantly check to determine how those students are progressing in order to adjust that plan. Those adjustments hopefully work to help students eventually hit that target. This book provides examples of what I call the "Assessment Target," which I connect with the differentiation framework proposed by Silver, Strong, and Perini (2007). This framework, which they base on

---

* For information about strategies for determining students' readiness, interests, and learning styles, and for suggestions for gathering content resources, see Northey (2005) or Waterman (2006). Also, for differentiating assessment ideas that address informal, preassessment, and summative assessment, see Waterman (2009).

the work of Jung (1923), suggests that students fall into one or more of four learning styles: mastery, understanding, self-expressive, and interpersonal. I show how to base an Assessment Target on one or more of these styles and also include learning styles from the *Multiple Intelligences* (Gardner, 1993), and from Dunn and Dunn (1993).

How Can We Link Assessment That Teachers Differentiate with Theories of Learning?

It is important to connect differentiated assessment with theories of learning. What follows shows how specific researchers suggest choosing assessment processes based on theory (adapted from Herman, Ashbacher, & Winters, 1992, pp. 18–20). I have added how that theory applies specifically to assessments teachers differentiate.

♦ *Theory:* We construct knowledge from our interactions with the world. We learn when we use our prior knowledge in combination with our experiences from which we create meaning.

Applying theory to differentiated assessment suggests teachers should:

- Assess students' discussions and conversations.

- Assess opportunities to show divergent thinking (multiple paths to answers that vary).

- Assess various ways of demonstrating learning.

- Assess critical thinking skills such as the highest levels of "New Bloom" (Anderson, Krathwohl, Airasian, Cruikshank, Mayer, Pintrich, Raths, & Wittrock, 2001).

- Assess students' connections to their own experiences and prior knowledge.

♦ *Theory:* Learning occurs at all ages and stages and it does not occur in a linear and sequential manner.

Applying theory to differentiated assessment suggests teachers should:

- Assess students at all ages and stages of development in problem solving.

- Not require mastery of basic skills prior to assessing students' abilities to have high-level discussions, solve complex problems, or demonstrate critical thinking.

♦ *Theory:* Students exhibit many and varied intelligences, learning styles, attention spans, ability to remember, aptitude, and developmental stages.

Applying theory to differentiated assessment suggests teachers should:

- Assess using a wide variety of tasks (not just reading and writing).

- Evaluate assessment products students choose.

- Allow enough time for complex assessment products.

- Allow time for students to think about their responses to assessments (do not use timed tests too often).

- Allow students to revise their work based on teacher and peer feedback.

- Address all learning styles when assessing learning.

♦ *Theory:* Students will be more likely to succeed on an assessment if they understand its goals, see representative models, and can compare their response to an excellent example.

Applying theory to differentiated assessment suggests teachers should:

- Discuss the goals of an assessment with students.
- Allow students to have input into what might represent standard and excellent responses to an assessment.
- Show students a variety of examples of responses to an assessment and discuss these examples with them..
- Allow time for self and peer evaluation of assessments.
- Make assessment criteria clear.

♦ *Theory:* Students' motivation, self-esteem, and the effort they exert affect their performance on and learning from any assessment.

Applying theory to differentiated assessment suggests teachers should:

- Relate assessment to students' real world interests and concerns.
- Encourage students to see the connection between the effort they make and the results of their performance on an assessment.

♦ *Theory:* Students learn well in social activities, such as in collaborative group work.

Applying theory to differentiated assessment suggests teachers should:

- Assess students as they work in groups.
- Assess using group products.
- Assess students as they perform different roles within the group.

♦ *Theory:* Determining how students are learning material while they are learning allows teachers to adjust instruction to meet students' needs.

Applying theory to differentiated assessment suggests teachers should:

- Assess students often and in many ways while they are learning (i.e., formative assessment).
- Provide prompt feedback on formative assessments so that students know how well they are learning.
- Adjust instruction based on results of formative assessments.
- Use summative assessment based on evidence from formative assessments.

What is *Formative* Assessment?

Formative assessment is any sampling of student ability *during* the learning process. This sampling is formative if it allows teachers to address the evidence of students' ability or lack of ability by adjusting instruction. Formative *assessment, evaluation,* and *feedback* work closely together. For instance, *assessment* is collecting or sampling students' work, *evaluation* is judging that work based on criteria, and *feedback* is letting students know specifically and accurately how well they did in comparison to that criteria. The criterion can be a "right" answer, a rubric, or a product guide, and students should have access to those criteria on which teachers plan to evaluate their work. This method of formative assessment is called criterion-referenced testing (or assessment). It is not to be confused with norm-based testing (or assessment), which measures students against the performance of other students.

Prompt and accurate feedback is highly important to the learning process, especially for the process of differentiated formative assessment. Research tells us that the closer the sampling is to the adjustment of instruction, the more effective it is in terms of student achievement. For example, Wiliam and Leahy (2007) suggest three *time scale cycles* for feedback on assessments: short, medium, and long. They define short as being any time between five seconds and one hour, medium as being between one day and two weeks, and long as being between four weeks and one year.

Short Time Scale Feedback Examples

When teachers check for understanding relatively soon after presenting a new idea, they are formatively assessing based on a short time scale. For example, teachers might explain a process (e.g., how to proceed with a lab, how to form groups) and immediately take an informal formative assessment from the class by asking for a thumbs up or thumbs down regarding whether students are ready to proceed. If any students put thumbs down, the teacher might call on a student with thumb up to explain the process again. Immediate feedback from students is crucial for moving forward; however, the success of this kind of formative assessment requires that teachers develop the kind of classroom culture in which students feel comfortable expressing their lack of understanding. For example, if any student thinks he or she might be ridiculed for not "getting it," this kind of formative assessment will not work well. Another short time scale for feedback is asking students to answer a few questions about the lesson at the end of the class. Their answers to these questions could serve as their "ticket out the door." Teachers can see from these responses if all students understood the lesson, if some students did not understand it, or if there are whole-class misconceptions. With this information, teachers can address learning problems during the next lesson or take aside certain students for additional help.

Medium Time Scale Examples

A medium time scale formative assessment could include next class pop or announced quizzes on the material covered in the previous class. For example, the "5 Question Quiz" (Waterman, 2009) is a great tool for measuring students' understanding of previous class material. Teachers might evaluate these quizzes during planning or after school to provide feedback for the next class, or they might evaluate them while students are engaged in non–teacher-led work, such as a reading, writing, or research workshop. Teachers evaluate these quizzes to determine what they may need to reteach to the entire class; if they need to take aside those who have not learned and reteach them in a separate or special group session; or if they need to tier another lesson on the topic using a cooperative learning activity grouped by readiness. Another example of medium time for feedback is a test (e.g., short answer or multiple choice) or writing assignment at the end of a discreet set of concepts. These kinds of assessments can be made formative if teachers allow students to retake other versions of the test of the concepts or if they allow students to revise their written responses. The research stresses the importance of specific and accurate feedback on student work making this strategy useful as a learning tool. One way to inspire students to do their best on the first try is to give extra credit if they do not need to take additional assessments. It is important to give students the grades they earn if they do the work again with more success. Giving students partial credit may not provide enough incentive.

Long Time Scale Examples

A formative assessment based on a long time for feedback could be a criterion-referenced or benchmark test of discreet learning objectives that the teacher or the district has determined. When students and teachers receive the results of these tests, teachers may regroup students for reteaching discreet learning objectives. One strategy is to regroup students for reteaching across classrooms so that the students might have the benefit of learning the material from another teacher. Another strategy is to use a homeroom period or a ninth block period to provide targeted instruction ranging from remediation to enrichment.

Summative Assessment

Summative assessment is also an example of a long time scale and should be reserved for the purpose of showing what students have learned; therefore, teachers should only use it when they have finished teaching a topic or when others, including students, parents, other teachers, administrators, and district leaders need to know the final results of the teaching and learning.

Figure 1.1 compares and contrasts formative and summative assessment using a Venn diagram.

Figure 1.1. Compare and Contrast Formative and Summative Assessment

Formative Assessment

For Learning

Short, medium, and long time scales

During learning

Informs instruction so that teachers might adjust it for optimal opportunities to learn

Both are ways to measure achievement

Summative Assessment

Of Learning

Medium and long time scales

After learning

Informs students and teachers of the final level of achievement

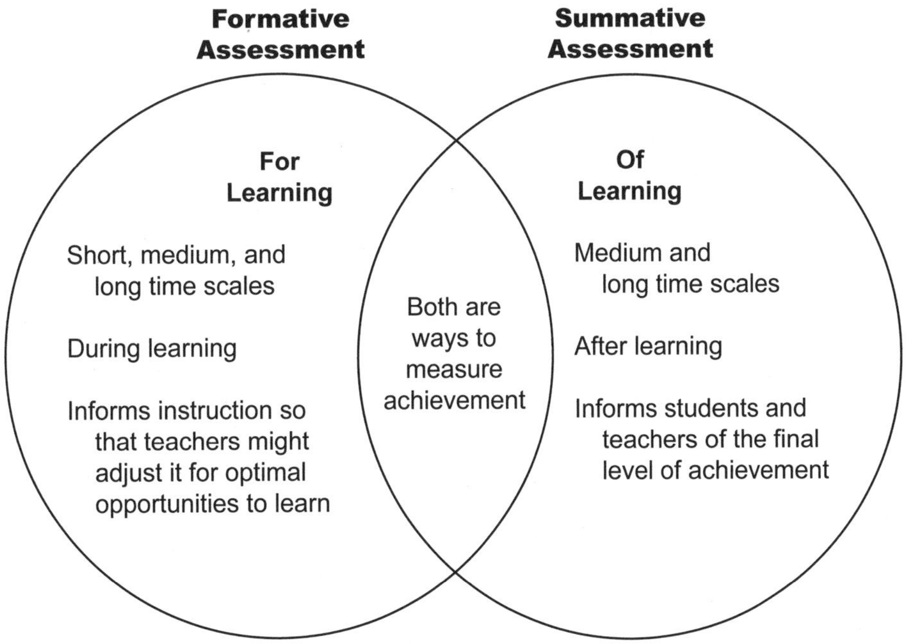

Formative Differentiated Assessments
That Are Fair, Valid, and Reliable

Those who construct standardized tests are required to carefully address issues of fairness, validity, and reliability. If they do not show that their assessments meet certain criteria, these assessments are unacceptable. Although classroom teachers are not required to subject their assessments to these kinds of requirements, if they do not make some effort to address them, students may not achieve at optimal levels. Addressing these three issues is also important if teachers want to create *common* differentiated formative assessments. Here are some suggestions to help teachers think about addressing these issues in their differentiated formative assessments:

1. *Fairness* addresses test bias and assures that the language and topics in the assessment do not discriminate against anyone based on race, gender or ethnic group. If teachers want to make sure their assessments are fair to everyone, they may want to ask colleagues who are a different gender, race, and/or from a different ethnic group to review their assessment to look for issues of bias. They might make it clear to this person that they realize that biases are often hidden from us and that they will not be offended if their colleague identifies potential problems with their assessment.

2. *Validity* means that the assessment measures what it says it will measure. For example, if teachers are trying to determine if students can solve multistep equations, their assessment might include word problems that require students to use multi step-equations. They would not give students word problems that only require one-step equations.

3. *Reliability* means that the assessment is consistent in various contexts and situations. For example, if teachers assess students in first period and they do well, but students in fifth period do not, they might question the reliability of their test.

Responding to Formative Assessments: <u>R</u>egroup, <u>R</u>eteach, <u>R</u>emediate, and En<u>R</u>ich

Teachers use formative assessments to adjust their responses to students as individuals, in groups, or as a whole class. For example, if teachers assess learning for a specific concept and the majority of the class shows lack of achievement, then these teachers should consider presenting the concept in a completely different manner (i.e., reteaching). If only a few students fail to grasp the concepts, teachers may choose to group them (i.e., regrouping) for some kind of reteaching while the rest of the class continues with learning activities that deepen their understanding of the concepts (i.e., enriching). If only one or two students do not understand the concept, the teachers may consider suggesting that these students come for after school or during school remediation (i.e., remediating).

In other words, the choices teachers make based on formative assessment of students' work can include regrouping, reteaching, remediating, *and* enriching.

Differentiated Formative Assessment Closely Connected to EEKs and KUDs and MOs

Most researchers and practitioners agree that the best unit planning begins with serious attention to the *Enduring Essential Knowledge* (EEK) that students must learn in their subject area (e.g., Physics, Algebra, Geometry). Most districts require their teachers to use their district or state curriculum *Standards,* and some teachers still rely heavily on their textbooks to help them determine what is essential within a topic or concept in that subject area. Having a clear idea of the essential ideas for a unit helps teachers write the *Essential Questions* (EQ) that assessments will address. These EQs will also help teachers appropriately address what students *Know, Understand,* and can *Do* (KUD) for that unit. Because these EEKs, EQs, and KUDs must be measured, teachers must state them as *Measurable Objectives* (MOs) that can actually provide best evidence that learning is taking place. To provide evidence of a learning-results orientation, teachers should design assessments that address the MOs that closely align with the Standards, EEKs, EQs, and KUDs. If they are not closely connected, they will appear to be a waste of precious time. Also, teachers must develop clear evaluation standards that they make available to students prior to the assessment. Teachers may present these standards to students in the form of rubrics, product guides, syllabi with point systems, or other information about how they will grade student work.

Differentiating Assessments Based on Learning Styles

Because teachers' learning styles often do not match their students' styles, it is important for teachers to do their best to accommodate all styles of learning as they assess it. Although it is a great idea to match students' learning styles with the way teachers assess them, unfortunately, learning styles assessments are not always reliable predictors of students' needs over time. Research tells us that students' learning styles vary from day to day based on their mood or events with which they are dealing. Also, many learning styles inventories are not normed for children and teens, and although it is important to consider learning styles, it is dangerous to assume that a students' learning style will be consistent over time; consequently, teachers should constantly assess students' learning preferences as they begin to explore a new topic of study.

Formatively Assessing If Students Understand

Teachers who take the time at the beginning of the year to get to know their students' learning styles are better equipped to design differentiated formative assessments. It also helps to look for signs of understanding. Reynolds, Martin, and Groulx (1995) suggest that there are seven "Indicators of Understanding" that teachers might look for as they keep constant note of where each student might be in the learning process. Students who are learning have the following traits:

1. *Demeanor:* They have a brightness of their eyes.

2. *Extension:* They take the idea and run with it.

3. *Modification:* They do not have to follow the rules or pattern; they can do their own thing.

4. *Context:* They see the same patterns and ideas in other places.

5. *Shortcuts:* They know the information so well that they can take shortcuts.

6. *Explanation:* They can explain the topic to someone else.

7. *Focus:* They stay focused on the topic for long periods of time.

Feedback Versus Grading

One of the most controversial aspects of differentiating assessment is how to make grading fair. If teachers do not assess and evaluate every student the same way, how can that be fair? Being fair when grading differentiated assessments brings to light the rationale for grading students at all. Many educators and researchers say that teachers should use grading sparingly as a means of determining how well students achieve on a predetermined standard. Also, *if grades are the only feedback* we give students about their work, then we are not using assessment to help students learn, we are using it in a *learning-stopping* way. What follows is a conceptual framework that shows the interaction among planning, assessment, evaluation, instruction, and feedback.

Designing Differentiated Assessments (Method 1)

To design differentiated formative assessments, teachers may use a process that is spiraling and interactive (Figure 1.2 illustrates this process) as follows:

A Spiraling Interaction of Planning, Assessment, Evaluation, Instruction, and Feedback

Phase 1: Preassessment

The teacher develops and administers a preassessment to determine the following:

♦ What *background knowledge* do students already have about this unit?

♦ How *ready* are these students to learn this material?

♦ What *learning styles* might students use to learn about this unit?

♦ What *interests* do students have to motivate them to learn about this unit?

♦ What *resources* do I need to help students access the information in this unit?

Preassessment is a critical step in designing differentiated assessments and the step that unit designers seem to most often leave out. Teachers who are eager to "get planned" for various reasons often fail to align their instruction and assessments with the needs of the students they teach. This assessment could be a simple written or oral survey. If teachers know what students already know, what they want to learn, how they want to learn it, and whether they are interested in it or not, they should have more success with the unit.

Phase 2: First Evaluation

Teachers must carefully evaluate this preassessment. Students quickly realize if their teacher is paying close attention to the assessment or merely checking it off.

Phase 3: Formative Planning

Based on what teachers learn from their preassessment, they should take the following steps for each unit of study:

♦ *Step 1:* Make a preliminary decision about what to teach based on the *Standard*.

Figure 1.2. Graphic of Spiraling Interaction of Planning, Instruction, Assessment, and Feedback

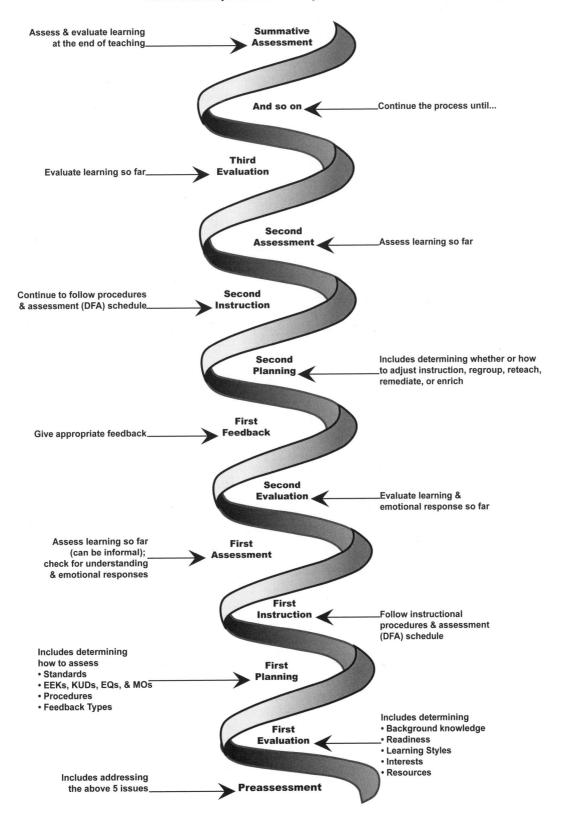

Assess & evaluate learning at the end of teaching ——→ **Summative Assessment**

And so on ←—— Continue the process until...

Evaluate learning so far ——→ **Third Evaluation**

Second Assessment ←—— Assess learning so far

Continue to follow procedures & assessment (DFA) schedule ——→ **Second Instruction**

Second Planning ←—— Includes determining whether or how to adjust instruction, regroup, reteach, remediate, or enrich

Give appropriate feedback ——→ **First Feedback**

Second Evaluation ←—— Evaluate learning & emotional response so far

Assess learning so far (can be informal); check for understanding & emotional responses ——→ **First Assessment**

First Instruction ←—— Follow instructional procedures & assessment (DFA) schedule

Includes determining how to assess
• Standards
• EEKs, KUDs, EQs, & MOs ——→ **First Planning**
• Procedures
• Feedback Types

First Evaluation ←—— Includes determining
• Background knowledge
• Readiness
• Learning Styles
• Interests
• Resources

Includes addressing the above 5 issues ——→ **Preassessment**

- ◆ *Step 2:* Determine the *Essential Enduring Knowledge* (EEK) and the *Essential Question(s)* (EQs) that reflect that Standard. (*Note:* Teachers might allow students to have input in this process.)

- ◆ *Step 3:* Specify the *Knowledge, Understanding,* and what students can *Do* (KUDs) that will answer that question(s) and address the goal or standard.

- ◆ *Step 4:* Specify *Procedures* that allow for a sequence of *Differentiated Formative Assessments* (DFAs) to use to determine best evidence of students' learning.

- ◆ *Step 5:* Plan the kind of feedback you or peers will give students at each step.

- ◆ *Step 6:* Examine your *Resources* to decide how you will scaffold or enrich, and find alternative differentiated resources so that every student will have access to materials on their instructional reading level. At the instructional reading level students cannot read independently and still need some help from the teacher or their peers, but they should not become frustrated.

Phase 4: First Differentiated Instruction

In most cases, teachers begin the unit by handing out the unit syllabus, which should include a statement of the Enduring Essential Knowledge and/or the Essential Questions, the Measurable Objectives, and a "proposed" schedule of learning activities and assessments. They begin instruction by using a differentiated method. Chapters 2 through 6 provide many examples of instructional strategies for this phase.

Phase 5: First Informal and Formative Assessment

During this phase it is essential that teachers consistently use *Differentiated Formative Assessments* that *check for understanding and for emotional responses.* As students experience new information and concepts, teachers should constantly use these assessments to check students' progress on measurable objectives and emotional connection to the learning (i.e., their motivation).

Phase 6: Second Evaluation

Teachers must evaluate assessments taken during class and after class. Teachers should avoid planning assessments if they do not make time to evaluate them. *Assessing without evaluating is useless and destructive to teacher accountability and ultimately does harm to the classroom culture.*

Phase 7: First Feedback

Evaluation that provides clear, accurate, and thorough feedback is one of the most important factors that determines learning or no learning. If teachers assess formative learning, they must provide correction and direction. It is also important to give feedback if a student responds negatively on affective (feeling-based) assessments. Using some one-on-one time with certain students may be critical for the well-being of that student and for the health of the whole class. Teachers might interact one-on-one with a student before school, during a working lunch, after school, or during times when the class is in workshop mode. Research shows that one-on-one time between teacher and student is extremely beneficial for relationship building. It is also important to provide individualized remedial instruction for some students. Many schools have prioritized creating this kind of service by using upper grade or honors students as peer coaches or using a special staff position. It would be sad if any student had to fail because the teacher or the school did not make it a point to find a way to help every child succeed.

Phase 8: Second Planning

It is essential that teachers go back to planning to adjust instruction and assessments that align with the learning needs of the class and of individual students. Students who have made great gains in mastering EQs, KUDs, and MOs need enrichment instruction to deepen their learning, and students who need more experience and practice need other instruction and assessment.

Continue this process as necessary until....

Last Phase: Summative Assessment

At this point, the teachers should have sufficiently differentiated instruction and assessments so that all students experience some level of success on the summative assessment. This assessment may be standardized or differentiated.

Designing a Differentiated Learning Progression (Method 2)

According to Popham (2008), the best way to design formative assessments is by determining a learning progression, which he said historically was known as a *task analysis*. He says that to know when and where to formatively assess students' learning, teachers need to develop a kind of outline of the learning process for a specific "curricular aim" (p. 24). Popham (2008) acknowledges that this progress may not always proceed in the same linear manner for all students; therefore, my adaptation shows how teachers might differentiate a learning progression. What follows is my adaptation of a generic differentiated learning progression. As part of that adaptation, I call the outline of the learning process the "Assessment Target" rather than the "Curriculum Aim."

♦ *Step 1:* Determine the "Assessment Target," which includes the "curriculum" and how it is differentiated. The outline is as follows:

Curriculum

1. Standard—Determined by the district or state.

2. Essential Question(s)—Represents the Essential Enduring Knowledge that the unit will address.

3. Know—The knowledge the student will gain from the unit.

4. Understand—The enduring understanding the student will gain from the unit.

5. Do—The skills the student will gain from the unit.

6. Measurable Objective(s)—The measure of student achievement regarding the "Assessment Target."

Differentiation

1. Readiness

2. Interests

3. Learning Styles

Curriculum

Standard—from the district or state	Essential Question(s)	Know	Understand that…	Do includes measurable objectives (see template below)

Measurable Objective(s) which includes the following parts:

a. Introduction	b. Thinking Verb(s)	c. Product	d. Response Criterion	e. Content

Differentiation

Readiness	Interests	Learning Styles

- *Step 2:* Teachers find out students' knowledge and readiness to begin addressing the "Assessment Target." Teachers must use preassessment strategies like K-W-L (What students <u>K</u>now, <u>W</u>hat they can do, and what they plan to <u>L</u>earn or how they will <u>L</u>earn it) (Ogle, 1986) or other means of answering this question. It is at this point that teachers begin to plan differentiation of the learning progression.

- *Step 3:* Teachers assign a differentiated task and group students appropriately.

- *Step 4:* Teachers assess students' knowledge and skills after they have completed their assigned task.

- *Step 5:* Teachers may regroup students based on the knowledge and skills they gain from accomplishing their assigned task. Teachers may also adjust the tasks they plan.

- *Step 6:* Teachers continue with this process until they have enough information to decide to administer a summative assessment to address the "Curriculum Aims."

Figure 1.3 shows a "Formative Assessment Cycle" and is adapted from McMillan (2007, p. 3).

Figure 1.3. Graphic of Formative Assessment Cycle

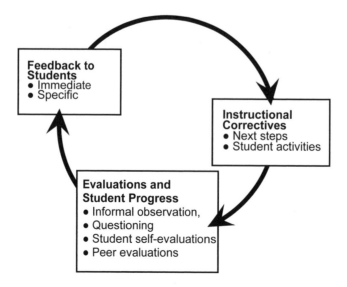

Types of Assessment

Looking at Assessment Examples Through the Lens of Assessing for Student Learning

The material in this section is based on Stiggins, Arter, Chappuis, and Chappuis (2007).

In Figure 1.4, teachers will find differentiated formative assessment ideas based on the Stiggins' model of matching assessment methods with achievement targets. The achievement targets include Knowledge Mastery, Reasoning Proficiency, Performance Skills, and Ability to Create Products.

Figure 1.4. Types of Assessment

Assessment Method	Formats	Targets that may be assessed
Selected Response + Easy to score + Can cover lots of material − Problems with guessing for most formats − Hard to develop effective ones	Multiple choice True–False Matching Fill-in-the-blank	♦ Knowledge Mastery—Easy to assess through this method. Used when there is one right answer. ♦ Reasoning Proficiency—Use item formulas to develop questions that address such reasoning skills as making inferences, predictions, comparing and contrasting, and making connections with and among texts.
Extended Written Response + Easy to develop − Time-consuming to score	Oral or Written Exercises (i.e., prompts or questions)	♦ Knowledge Mastery—Can assess extensive volumes of knowledge. ♦ Reasoning Proficiency—Can also assess reasoning targets. The critical factor is the development of the evaluation method (e.g., rubric).
Performance Assessment + Can assess many learning targets − Can be biased or inaccurate	Two parts: Tasks and Performance Criteria	♦ Reasoning Proficiency ♦ Performance Skills ♦ Ability to Create Products ♦ Knowledge Mastery
Personal Communication + Can assess many learning targets − Can be biased or inaccurate	♦ Instructional questions and answers ♦ Class discussions ♦ Student conferences and interviews ♦ Journals and logs ♦ Oral examination	♦ Knowledge Mastery ♦ Reasoning Proficiency—Can elicit answers to questions from categories such as analyzing, comparing and contrasting, synthesizing, classifying, inferring or deducing, and evaluating. ♦ Performance Skills

General Assessment Ideas

What follows is a list of ideas that might be useful as teachers plan differentiated formative assessments for students.

Vocabulary Self-Assessment

One of the most important aspects of reading comprehension for learning is the students' levels of vocabulary knowledge. Students often fail to grasp important content if they are unfamiliar with critical terms related to that content. A vocabulary preassessment (Figure 1.5) may help teachers better plan their method of teaching. You can use this template as a seat activity or use it as a kinesthetic activity by calling out the word and asking students to go to one side of the room if they know the word or to the other side if they do not. You should then quiz the students on that knowledge. Forced responses are better than volunteer responses to make sure students truly know the word.

Figure 1.5. Vocabulary Self-Assessment

Vocabulary Self-Assessment Template

We are learning about_____. Here are some words you need to know to understand this topic. Look carefully at each of these words to determine if you have a working knowledge of any or all of them. Put a ✓ in the column if you agree and do what the category asks you to do. You will check your answers using a dictionary. If you were correct, put a ✓ in the "Yes" column. If you were wrong, make the necessary corrections.

Teacher supplies the words in the boxes in this column	Word (Looks familiar; I can say it)	I can write a definition	I can use it in a sentence	Yes

Visualizing Assessment

This strategy allows students to use pictures to capture what they understand about information that might preview a unit of study. The teacher should caution students to refrain from laughing at anyone's drawings. This assessment will not work if the teacher has not created a safe atmosphere for students' sharing. This assessment can help teachers determine what students find important and what they understand as they begin a unit of study.

- *Step 1:* Hand out a sheet of long white paper to each student and ask them to divide it into four or six boxes, depending on the level of the class. Provide colored pencils, markers, or crayons if possible.

- *Step 2:* Read information to students and ask them to draw pictures of what they are hearing. It could be, for example, a story, a process, or an event. Check to see that everyone has drawn something. This is differentiated formative assessment (DFA) #1.

- *Step 3:* Ask students to trade papers with a partner. Ask them to label their partner's papers without talking. This is DFA #2.

- *Step 4:* After partners have labeled each others' work, they should discuss the labeling and make corrections.

- *Step 5:* Partners present their drawings and labels. This is DFA #3.

- *Step 6:* Teachers (or students) write seminar questions about the drawings and have a seminar about the story, process, or event. This is DFA #4.

Kinesthetic Assessments

Teachers can use shower curtains or mark the floor with tape to create kinesthetic games that students can play. They can take any fact-based information to the kinesthetic assessment level by dividing students into teams and creating spaces like corners of the room, floor-sized game boards (like chess or checkers), sitting and standing at desks, or being in the line or out of it. Here is a kinesthetic board game suggestion:

- *Twister*—Teachers may make or purchase a *Twister* game. They should make questions that match the colors on the game board. Four students stand on each edge of the game board and one student is in charge of working the color wheel and asking the questions (making five students per group). When a student misses a question, the student must move a hand or foot to the color of the question. Students who correctly answer the question do not have to move. The student left standing at the end of the game is the winner. Teachers could use this assessment with five students at a time while others rotate in or observe, or they could have a game for several groups of five.

Tactual Assessments

Teachers may use a variety of assessment strategies that require students to use simply constructed learning tools that appeal to students who learn best by using their hands (tactual learners). Cardboard shapes or file folders, string, markers and punched holes or cutout shapes can make interesting and creative fact-based quizzes for tactual learners. All of these tools can be made to be "self-correcting" so that students might use them on their own as a formative self-assessment to review for a summative assessment. What follows is an example of an easy-to-construct informal tactual assessment tool to help students and teachers determine if students have learned facts and concepts in any unit of study.

- *Flip Chute* (Milgram, Dunn, & Price, 2009; also, see Dunn & Dunn, 1993)

  - Construct the chute from a milk carton.

  - Next make small cards (about the size of a business card) that have questions on one side and answers on the other. Students read the question to themselves, to a partner, or in a group. They say what they think the answer is and then put the card in the chute. When the card comes out of the chute, the students access the answer. Students could just turn the card over to see the answer, but putting it in the chute makes finding the answer more enjoyable for these learners.

Oral Examinations

Teachers might use oral assessments as formative or summative examinations. Here are the steps for oral examinations (based on Stiggins et al., 2007):

♦ *Step 1:* Teachers write high-level questions that focus on what they want students to know about the unit and the reasoning skills they want them to demonstrate. Then teachers make sure they are actually assessing content and reasoning rather than verbal facility.

♦ *Step 2:* Teachers determine a fair method of evaluating the oral performance. This could include the following:

- Ask questions using language that all students can understand. Do not let language use become an obstacle for students' showing what they know and can do. Also, be prepared to differentiate questions for students who have language difficulties or learning difficulties.

- Have "best answers" written and some idea of what might constitute other acceptable answers. Be sure that qualified experts in the field would agree with what you have determined to be an acceptable versus a quality answer.

♦ *Step 3:* Teachers should use a fair method of determining who answers what question. It could be drawing names out of a basket or another random method.

♦ *Step 4:* Teachers should have an evaluation method (e.g., a checklist, rating scale) in hand as they begin the oral examination. They should consider videotaping or audiotaping the examination so that they can truly be fair in their evaluation of students' answers.

♦ *Step 5:* Teachers should create an atmosphere of seriousness as opposed to one that is stressful, and make it clear that blurting answers is unacceptable. They should present questions to the entire class and not let students choose the questions they answer.

Seven Types of Presentation Assessments

Teachers may use presentations as formative or summative assessments of students' learning. Figure 1.6 is a list of seven types of presentations from Silver, Strong, and Perini (2007).

Crossword Puzzle Assessments

An interesting way to assess students' vocabulary learning is by creating or having students create a crossword puzzle with the proper names or terms from any unit of study. Teachers or students may easily produce these puzzles (and others) by going online to access a wealth of free puzzle makers. One site that is easy to use is http://www.puzzle-maker.com/CW/ (retrieved June 24, 2009). Either the teacher or students can access this site. The teacher or student types in the name or term followed by the slash mark (/), and then the definition. The site allows the typing in of a large or small number of names or terms with their definitions. Here are some hints to help teachers make best puzzles:

- If teachers or students are using a proper name or phrase that includes spaces, they should not put a space between the words unless they tell students that there will be blank boxes on the puzzle. The puzzle maker will put a box for every space before the slash mark.

Figure 1.6. Seven Types of Presentation Assessments

Type	Purpose	Assessment Criteria
Recount	To explain what happened.	Accurately explains the sequence of events with appropriate main ideas and details.
Instruction	To present or demonstrate a specific skill.	Clearly explains how to perform the skill.
Narrative	To entertain, inform, or share thoughts with an audience.	Explains information in an entertaining way.
Information report	To explain a topic.	Presents information in a complete and organized way.
Explanation	To identify causes and effects.	To explain "why" rather than "what" through reasoning.
Argument	To take a position and support it.	Takes a position and supports it with evidence and counterarguments.
Inquiry	To develop a project through the process of research.	Supports a well-conceived hypothesis with a variety of sources to support it.

Source: Silver, Strong, & Perini, 2007, p. 33.

- Teachers and students should double check their spelling because there is no spellcheck to alert the person making the puzzle that they might be spelling the word incorrectly. Spelling words correctly is *essential* for crossword puzzles.

- If the puzzle maker does not include a word list from which students might choose the words that they should use in the puzzle, the teacher might want to include a list of the words.

Kinds of Portfolios to Capture Assessment Data

Portfolios are collections of student work that can be assessed. Figure 1.7 (page 18) is a list of the kinds of portfolios described by Stiggins et al. (2007).

Feedback

Teachers' feedback is a critical factor affecting the usefulness of differentiated formative assessments. According to Ramaprasad (1983), feedback provides information about "a gap between" a student's work as it stands and the work as it might be if it matched all the criteria for highest achievement (p. 4). He says that ultimately the student has to understand how to close that gap and to decide to do what it takes to close it. Feedback from the teacher will not help if the student decides to ignore it. In a similar vein, Kluger and DeNisi (1996) say that feedback only serves a formative purpose if it allows students to alter their work so that they can achieve the learning objective(s) at levels to which they aspire or that are more in line with criteria. Feedback serves little purpose if students cannot use it to improve their work and their grade or points for the work.

Figure 1.7. Portfolio Types

Project Portfolios	Focuses on the work from a specific project, shows evidence that the student has effectively completed the project, and shows that all the steps have been accomplished appropriately. Students may annotate their artifacts or write a process paper explaining their response.
Growth Portfolios	Students show the process of their growth in an area of learning. They select representative work about which they write reflections focusing on their growth. The challenge is to make sure students choose representative work.
Achievement Portfolios	Students choose work that represents their achievement on learning targets at certain points and on the course of study. Students annotate their work to show that they have responded accurately to these targets. They must include an appropriate number of samples of the learning so that it is clear that their work has been sustained over a period of time.
Competence Portfolios	Provides evidence that the student has achieved competence in an area of study. It is similar to achievement portfolio, but is most interested in providing evidence of mastery.
Celebration Portfolios	Students choose certain work to present to the class as a way of celebrating their success.

Note: Portfolios are different from work folders, which are only places to hold the students' work.

Teachers need to remember when they give feedback that it should be as nonjudgmental—negatively *or* positively—as possible, and that feedback should be detailed so that students know how they might correct their errors. Just knowing that something is wrong does not help student achievement (Bangert-Drowns, Kulik, Kulik, & Morgan, 1991).

Student motivation is negatively affected if feedback is punitive. Teachers need to use feedback to inspire rather than shut down learning. A good way to tell if you are using feedback correctly is if all students are engaged and achieving.

Oral Feedback

There are several reasons for keeping oral feedback neutral rather than evaluative in either a positive or negative direction. The most important reason is that when teachers respond to individual students, the other students in the class are observing that response. Whatever teachers say to individual students, either positive or negative, has an effect on the rest of the class. Most teachers understand and acknowledge the damage negative feedback can cause, but they forget that positive feedback can also cause problems for those observing it. When a teacher highly praises a student's response, others who may feel inclined to respond may change their minds out of fear that their ideas will not be as highly acclaimed. Also, students' peers can penalize them if teachers overpraise them. The safest type of oral feedback is a specific response like, "Thank you for sharing an example of one of the primary causes of infectious diseases," or

"Thank you for providing the correct definition of that term. Knowing what it means will help us better understand that sentence."

Oral Formative Assessment Example: Formative Assessment Conversations

The primary goal of this kind of assessment is to allow students to learn how and to practice the art of reflecting on their work. The teacher should create a space for this process by inviting cordial participation and by helping students learn how to think and respond critically in an affirming rather than discounting manner. Teachers set the tone for this kind of exchange among students by showing them how to avoid empty praise and hurtful criticism.

- *Step 1:* Ask students to select an example of something they are working on (e.g., a piece of writing or a project artifact, such as a poster or script for a skit).

- *Step 2:* In small groups, with a partner, or in a whole-group setting (which is least preferred if the class is large), ask students to take turns talking about that work using the following kind of framework:

  - Explain the purpose of the piece and why you decided to create it.

  - Explain how the piece helped you learn the curriculum objective it is addressing (such as how it helped to answer the Essential Questions from the unit).

  - Explain any other issues relevant to the piece and what you have left to do.

  - Ask your partner, members of your small group, or the class (depending on your specific setting), (a) if they have any questions and (b) if they have any suggestions that might help you perfect the work.

  Note: At the end of each student's presentation, the teacher might suggest that those who are giving feedback give the student who is presenting at least one positive comment about the work. The teacher might need to model how to give specific positive feedback by taking some time to model and practice. The teacher might explain that "I like it" is not as useful as "The way you said _____ was interesting to me because (for example) you gave us lots of details about why you think you have the best idea about how to solve the problem." Some teachers call a strategy similar to this PQP (Praise, Question, Perfect).

- *Step 3:* Students use the information from these conversations to improve their work if they choose.

- *Alternative:* The teacher might also have these conversations individually with students when they are nearing completion of a piece of work or during all stages of the work. If the class is in workshop mode for working on projects, these kinds of formative assessment conversations can be continuous. (The term *assessment conversation* comes from the work of Ross & Mitchell, 1993; however, the process described here is my adaptation.)

Written Feedback

When teachers write comments, they should keep them neutral. A useful strategy is to write ideas in the form of questions, such as, "Should you add more examples of the symptoms of infectious diseases?" It is always a good idea to offer specific ideas about the strengths as well as the weaknesses of the students' work.

Feelings and Beliefs about Topic

Affective Domain Assessment

According to brain-based research, students learn more if teachers design learning activities that engage them emotionally; consequently, it is important to determine how students are feeling about a topic of study and how they are learning about that topic. The best ways to assess the affective domain are through survey or open written responses, such as in journals or learning logs. It is important to regularly check with students to make sure they are affectively engaged in the unit. See the following two ideas:

Surveys (Likert Scale)

A teacher who wants to know how students feel about a topic before presenting it may want to develop a survey. Teachers can also use this same survey to assess affective domain at the end of the unit of study.

Here is how to construct a Likert scale:

- ♦ *Step 1:* Decide what you want to measure. Because this scale tests only one dimension at a time, the concept you are considering must also be one-dimensional, for example, *the level of emotional involvement* students feel toward a unit of study.

- ♦ *Step 2:* Generate items. The students taking this survey must be able to rate items on a 1 to 4, 1 to 5, or 1 to 7 Agree or Disagree scale. If you want to know how students feel about a topic as they begin the unit, ask them to rate their emotional involvement on the lesson's main topics.

- ♦ *Step 3:* Administer the survey using the following scale:

1 = Strongly disagree

2 = Disagree

3 = Undecided

4 = Agree

5 = Strongly agree

Teachers can use an even number of responses to force a choice; however, they may want to give students a chance to take a neutral stance.

- ♦ *Step 4:* Get the final score. The final score for a respondent is the sum of his/her ratings for all of the items.

Here is a sample question:

1. I am interested in this topic. (*State the topic.*)				
1–Strongly disagree	2–Disagree	3–Undecided	4–Agree	5–Strongly agree

Another idea is to use a website called www.surveymonkey.com, which prompts teachers to design surveys on various topics. Keep in mind that developing a valid and reliable survey is a complex process involving statistical procedures; therefore, a classroom-developed survey usually will not generalize to other populations.

Journaling and Learning Logs

One of the best ways to assess the affective domain of students' learning about a unit of study is to ask them to write reflectively about that unit in a Journal or Learning Log.

Teachers should take the following steps to implement Learning Logs in the classroom:

♦ *Step 1:* Discuss reflective writing with students. Tell them it is about verbalizing thoughts and feelings through writing. If the students have had no experience with reflective writing, you may need to model it for them by writing a short reflection from your own experience with a topic.

♦ *Step 2:* Tell students that they should either keep a Learning Log in a special section of their notebooks or use a special journaling notebook. Emphasize to students the importance of reflecting about what they are learning on a regular basis, and that they are evaluating how much they have learned or not learned, so that they can maximize learning.

♦ *Step 3:* Make the time spent writing about learning an important activity by regularly scheduling two to ten minutes for journal or log writing at least twice per week. Emphasize that this kind of writing is informal and nonthreatening. Inform students that you will read the logs on a regular basis and respond to what students have written when possible.

♦ *Step 4:* Make learning logs and journals an important assessment tool in the classroom, and adjust teaching plans as necessary based on what students write about in their logs.

Other uses for Learning Logs:

♦ Reflecting on a unit of study to review for a test.

♦ Explaining how learning has changed ideas or misconceptions.

♦ Clarifying issues, especially if they are confusing.

♦ Summarizing ideas.

♦ Previewing or predicting what will be presented next.

♦ Recording data from experiential activities.

These ideas are from Northey (2005) and Fulwiler (1980).

Common Formative Assessments

Professional Learning Communities rely on common formative assessments to help teachers who teach the same subjects at the same grade level assess students' learning. These common assessments not only help teachers evaluate students, but they also help them evaluate their teaching. Teachers need to closely align their common assessments with Standards, EEKs and KUDS that they determine cooperatively. These assessments can be formative if these teachers adjust their instruction based on the results. Common assessments allow teachers to regroup students across teams and among teachers. For example, if three teachers assess students' ability to solve science problems based on the Periodic Table, they might find that certain students are not proficient in certain aspects of problem solving in this area, such as finding the atomic weight of a substance. The common assessment shows that all but two of Teacher A's students did well on finding atomic weight, but Teachers B and C had several students who did not do well in that area. These three teachers might decide together that Teacher A will reteach all of the students who are not proficient from all three classes how to figure atomic weight. The other two teachers may address another weak area if one emerges or they might develop enrichment activities that deepen and extend student learning about the Periodic Table.

Before administering the assessment, these three teachers should have not only co-constructed the assessment, but they should have also determined the criteria for scoring the work, especially if the assessment is a constructed response rather than a one-right-answer assessment. If they administer a constructed response assessment, the process becomes more complex. Ainsworth and Viegut (2007) suggest eight steps teachers might take together to score students' work. They say that taking these steps will increase the validity and reliability of their assessments.

Evaluating Student Work Collaboratively

Ainsworth and Viegut (2006) suggest that collaborative teams of teachers do the following:

- *Step 1:* Become familiar with the following assessment terms:
    - *Anchor papers*, which are student papers that represent each of the basic scores on the rubric. For example a 1 paper (lowest), a 2 paper, a 3 paper, and a 4 paper (highest). (*Note:* An anchor paper can be a science lab, a research report, or a mathematics proof.)
    - *Range Finder* papers, which are those that fall between the major numbers. For example 2.5 or 2+.
    - *Double scoring*, which is having two people score the assessment.
    - *Calibration*, which represents agreement among scorers concerning the rubric score.
    - *Adjacent score*, which is when two scorers have a 1 point difference between their scores. For example Scorer A gives the paper a 3 and Scorer B gives it a 4.
    - *Discrepant scores*, which is a 2 or more point-spread between scorers. For example, Scorer A gives the paper a 3 and Scorer B gives it a 1.
    - *Interrater reliability*, which is when two or more scorers agree on the score.
- *Step 2:* Reexamine the criteria that the team established in view of student responses. Make revisions of criteria that seem too subjective and that seem problematic in terms of reaching a consensus.
- *Step 3:* Read through student responses and select anchor and range finder papers to use in Step 4.
- *Step 4:* Have a practice session to make sure the team agrees on the anchor and range finder papers and how to reach agreement by referencing the rubric as a guide.
- *Step 5:* Begin scoring, keeping the anchor papers, range finder papers and the rubric as guides.
- *Step 6:* Double score papers, which is also known as having a "read behind," to address interrater reliability.

♦ *Step 7:* Work out a system to have a third person score if any scores are discrepant.

♦ *Step 8:* Record scores.

(Adapted from Ainsworth & Viegut, 2006, pp. 86–87.)

This process is most useful as a formative process if teachers examine scores recorded at Step 8 to note patterns. For example, if teachers' classes are mostly equal (e.g., one teacher does not have all the gifted or advanced students) and Teacher A's students score very well on the assessment, but several of teacher B's students scored below standard and some of Teacher C's students scored below standard, Teachers B and C may want to find out what Teacher A might be doing that works. The teachers might also regroup students so that Teacher A reteaches them.

Looking Together at Student Work

Another idea about collaboratively evaluating students' work is through a process of using protocols as a guide (McDonald, Mohr, Dichter, & McDonald, 2007; Blythe, Allen, & Powell, 1999). These authors suggest five kinds of questions that a collaborative team might ask as they formatively assess student work. They should ask questions about…

1. Quality of the work

    • Is it good enough?

    • What standard represents good enough?

    • How does this work achieve or not achieve the standard?

2. Teaching

    • What does the student work tell us about the quality of the assignment?

    • What kind of scaffolding helps promote a high-quality performance?

3. Understanding

    • How does this work show student understanding?

    • What understanding is just beginning?

4. Growth

    • How does this work show the student's growth?

    • What kind of scaffolding most effectively supports growth?

5. Intent

    • How does this work show the student's questions or concerns?

    • What parts of the assignment most engage the student's curiosity?

    • On which part of the assignment do the students work the hardest?

    • What is it about the assignment that challenges the student the most?

These authors suggest that collaborative teams use either of two methods to collaboratively evaluate student work: (a) the tuning protocol, which Joseph McDonald and David Allen (Allen, 1998; McDonald, 1996) developed, or (b) the Collaborative Assessment Conference, which Steve Seidel and Harvard's Project Zero Colleagues developed (Seidel et al., 1996).

Tuning Protocol

The tuning protocol (Blythe et al., 1999, p. 29) is a useful way to develop consensus standards that support instruction and improve the evaluation of students' projects. It is based on the idea that looking carefully, which takes quite a bit of time, at one or more student products, helps teachers set the standard for evaluating student products that are identical or similar to the one the team is evaluating. The "tuning" comes from evaluators offering "warm" or "cool" responses to students' artifacts in the context of a meeting. Teachers introduce samples of a student's or a small number of students' artifacts and the criteria on which they were based. They also present any other pertinent information, such as student or peer reflections, that further describe them. A brief adapted view of the process is a follows:

♦ *Step 1:* A facilitator provides an overview of the process and makes sure everyone introduces himself or herself. (10 minutes)

♦ *Step 2:* A teacher first presents a student's artifact, how it was assigned, and the rubric on which it was based, and then poses a guiding question to the group. For example: What learning goals does this artifact appear to address? (20 minutes)

♦ *Step 3:* Group members ask clarifying questions that the facilitator places in a warm or cool feedback category. (5 minutes)

♦ *Step 4:* The group examines the artifact that might be a copy or the original. Examples of artifacts include writing samples, video clips, and artwork. (15 minutes)

♦ *Step 5:* Group members reflect on how they will respond to the work. (2–3 minutes)

♦ *Step 6:* Group members share warm and cool feedback. The facilitator helps the group stay focused on the teacher's guiding question. (15 minutes)

♦ *Step 7:* Group members are silent while the teacher-presenter responds to the feedback. The facilitator holds the group accountable for staying within the protocol. (15 minutes)

♦ *Step 8:* The facilitator leads a debriefing discussion of the process. (10 minutes)

Collaborative Assessment Conference

This collaborative assessment conference (Seidel, Walters, Kirby, Olff, Powell, Scripp, & Veenema, 1996, pp. 33–34) is useful as a method of improving teaching practices by evaluating students' learning goals and issues, and noting the strengths and needs of a specific student. The process involves describing a student's work and wondering about the problems or concerns about which the student might have been most focused in developing the work. The conditions under which the work was developed are not available until after the group has examined it and thought about it. This process is best used to evaluate one or two open-ended works from a student's portfolio, but it may also be used with many samples.

What follows is an adapted overview of the process:

♦ *Step 1:* The group chooses a facilitator who will uphold the integrity of the process. The presenting teacher displays or provides copies of the work that the group will evaluate individually and silently. They should have paper and pencil available to make notes to themselves about the work.

- *Step 2:* The facilitator next asks this question: "What do you see?" Responses at this point should be nonjudgmental, but if evaluative comments do emerge, the facilitator should ask the person expressing the judgment to explain the evidence on which he or she bases that remark.

- *Step 3:* The facilitator asks participants: "What questions does this work raise for you?" Participants ask the presenting teacher questions, which he or she records, but does not answer.

- *Step 4:* The facilitator asks participants: "What do you think [the student] is working on?" The participants suggest problems or concerns the student might have had as he or she performed the task.

- *Step 5:* The facilitator invites the presenting teacher to speak about the student's work. He or she may answer any of the participants' questions, make comments about the context of the work, and express any surprises or unexpected responses about the work.

- *Step 6:* The facilitator invites all participants, including the presenting teacher, to discuss what this process and this work taught him or her about ways to support this particular student in future instruction.

- *Step 7:* The group reflects on the process as a whole.

- *Step 8:* The facilitator thanks everyone for participating.

Problem-Based Learning Formative Assessments

When students work together to practice solving a problem, the process fits within the category of formative assessment. When a teacher or an outside evaluator gives students a problem to solve to evaluate their ability to solve a problem, the assessment becomes summative. To make problem solving formative, teachers should assess student learning at each step toward solving the problem; the teacher should assess and then evaluate the learning that is occurring. Solving problems allows teachers to authentically assess students' construction of new learning, but they should be sure to determine specific measurable objectives or the learning could be happenstance or minimal.

How to Use This Book

In this book, I have leveled the examples of differentiated formative assessment as follows: Level 1—struggling learners, Level 2—typical learners, Level 3—gifted or highly advanced learners. See Waterman (2009) for more discussion of these levels designated as "at-risk students," "regular students," and "gifted or highly advanced students." I have provided examples for mathematics and science for these different readiness levels and have included different interests and learning preferences within differentiated learning strategies based on the work of Silver, Strong, and Perini (2007). If teachers would like to determine students' learning style based on this model, they should refer to Figure 6.8, "Choose Your Style Checklist," page 120. I have also noted when the strategy provides an opportunity for formative differentiated assessment. I will use the abbreviation DFA and a number (e.g., #1) to designate how many times teachers can formatively assess learning using the strategy.

Assessment Target

In Waterman (2009) I used the template shown in Figure 1.9 to show how teachers can write a plan for differentiating formative assessment.

Figure 1.9. Generic Template for Assessment Target

Curriculum				
Standard— from the district or state	**Essential Question(s):** The most important concept from a unit of study or lesson	**Know** Information teachers want students to have by the end of the unit or lesson	**Understand that...** Teachers should determine at least one idea or concept that represents the most important aspects of the unit.	**Do** What teachers want students to be able to do and including a measurable objective, which is broken down into 5 parts. See MO below
Measurable Objectives				
Introduction	**Thinking Verbs**	**Product**	**Response Criterion**	**Content**
Students will…	These verbs come from taxonomy of cognitive behavior. The ones I use are from "New Bloom."	What teachers want students to produce during or at the end of the unit or lesson.	The level of achievement clearly stated as an expectation of proficiency.	The topical information from the unit or lesson.
Differentiation				
Readiness Addresses how teachers might level the lesson for struggling, typical, or gifted learners.		**Interests** Addresses how teachers might use students' interests to inspire learning about the topic.		**Learning Styles** Lists the learning and thinking styles the assessment addresses.

For this book, I do not break down the parts in a template; instead, I write the information in outline form. What follows is an example of the new format from the first learning strategy in Chapter 2: "Assessment Target for New American Lecture Example: Graphing Linear Equations."

Assessment Target for New American Lecture
Example: Graphing Linear Equations

Curriculum
Standard: from the district or state
Essential Question: How do linear equations help us graph real-world problems?
Know: (Levels 1, 2, and 3) System of linear equations; how to collaborate. (Level 3) How to create and present a New American Lecture that applies understanding of graphing linear equations.
Understand that: Linear equations help us solve real-world math problems.
Do: (Levels 1, 2, and 3) Reflect on information for the system of linear equations; graph data generated by linear equations; interact with the teacher's lecture; collaborate with a partner. (Level 3) Create and present a New American Lecture applying ideas about linear equations.
Measurable Objective: (Levels 1, 2, and 3) Students will exemplify, generate, and classify in order to produce short written and spoken answers that accurately answer the questions prompted by the teacher's lecture about graphing linear equations. (Levels 1, 2, and 3) Students will exemplify, classify, and generate in order to produce graphs that accurately reflect data from linear equations. (Level 3) Students will exemplify, generate, classify, and create in order to produce a New American Lecture that is accurate and sufficient that applies their knowledge of how to graph linear equations.

Differentiation
Readiness: (Level 1) Present information that is on students' instructional reading level; pause more often; spend more time in whole-class discussion of information. (Level 2) Think-Pair-Share (Lyman, 1981) helps to scaffold. (Level 3) Create a New American Lecture with a partner or in small group.
Interests: Working with a partner and being able to interact with the teacher's instruction rather than passively listening can make learning more interesting.
Learning Styles: Mastery, interpersonal, understanding, and self-expression, mathematical/logical, analytical

Summary

This chapter defines differentiation and assessment and then explains how to make that differentiated assessment formative. It also explains the connection between learning theory and differentiated assessment. Next the chapter provides two designs for planning differentiated formative assessment: one using a spiraling planning process and the other using an "Assessment Target," which includes the curriculum and how it is differentiated. The chapter explains the perspectives of Stiggins et al. (2007) regarding types of assessment, provides ten general assessment ideas, and provides suggestions for common assessments. What follows in the next chapters includes specific "Assessment Target" ideas based on Silver, Strong, and Perini's (2007) concept of learning styles: mastery-based, understanding-based, self-expressive–based, and interpersonal-based assessments.

2
Mastery-Based Differentiated Formative Assessments

This chapter provides leveled examples of embedding formative assessment into a specific differentiated instructional strategy called mastery-based learning. According to Silver, Strong, and Perini (2007), mastery-based instructional strategies focus primarily on addressing students' ability to remember and summarize. Students who learn best this way are motivated by its clarity, sequencing, and quick feedback.

In addition, Guskey (2007, p. 70) explains that the mastery learning instructional process flows as follows (Figure 2.1): (a) start with unit goals, (b) use a formative assessment, (c) send students who master the assessment to *enrichment*, (d) send students who do not master for *correctives*, and (e) use another formative assessment. Continue this process until mastery. Use a summative assessment to evaluate unit goals at the end of the process.

Figure 2.1. The Mastery Learning Instructional Process

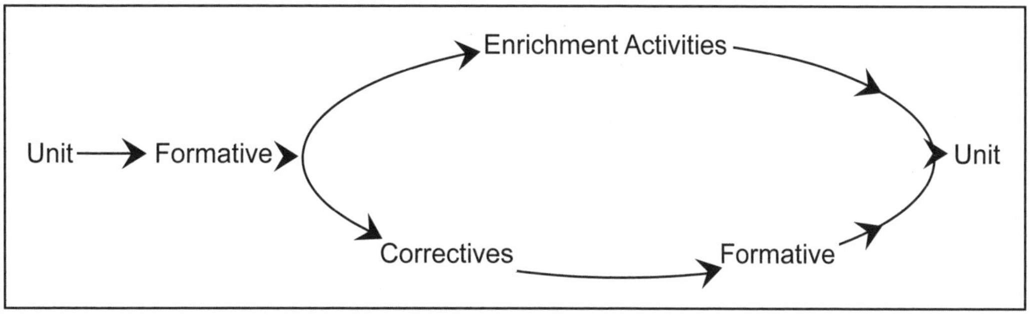

New American Lecture

The New American Lecture comes from the work of Ausubel (1963, 1968) as adapted by Silver, Strong, and Perini (2007). Teachers can use this instructional method to develop a sequence of formative assessments. Notice that teachers should plan backwards, so that the *first planned* differentiated formative assessment (DFA #3) is the *last implemented one*, and the *last planned* differentiated formative assessment (DFA #1) is the *first implemented one*. Here are the steps for designing this kind of lesson:

♦ *Step 1:* Choose a topic that you would like to present via lecture. Divide the information into chunks that will take you about five minutes or less to present orally to students. You might deliver the information in a PowerPoint presentation.

♦ *Step 2:* Create a visual organizer to help students keep track of the information you are presenting. Examples of organizers include compare/contrast organizers, flowcharts, sequence organizers, cycle organizers, fishbone organizers, topic organizers. Teachers can google "graphic organizers" to find free downloadable organizers. Go to http://www.educationplace.biz/graphicorganizer/ for a website from Houghton Mifflin Harcourt (retrieved December 10, 2008) that has more than thirty-five graphic organizers in English and in Spanish. Teacher evaluation of the organizer students complete during the lecture provides a formative assessment. This is DFA #3.

♦ *Step 3:* Write differentiated formative assessment questions that you will ask when you pause after no more than five minutes of lecturing. You should use a variety of question stems that allow students to experience the topic in different ways. Here are some examples of formative assessment question stems and prompts based on learning styles:

Mastery

1. Summarize what you have learned so far about….

2. Explain what you have seen and heard so far about….

3. Restate in your own words what you have learned about….

4. What are the most important points you have heard so far about…?

5. Without looking at your notes, what can you remember about…?

Understanding

1. What are the similarities and differences between…?

2. What do you think caused…?

3. What information have you learned that proves…?

Interpersonal

1. What feelings do you have so far about…?

2. Which part of…is hardest? Easiest?

3. Act out what you have learned so far about….

Self-Expression

1. Create a metaphor for….

2. Design a symbol for….

3. What would happen if…?

Answering these questions orally or in writing during the lecture is DFA #2.

♦ *Step 4:* Create a hook that will motivate students with all learning styles to become interested in the topic. This step also can be a way to formatively assess affective (i.e., emotional) engagement. What follows is a list of possible hooks based on learning styles:

1. *Mastery:* Get with a partner and co-create a list of everything you know about….

2. *Understanding:* Look at these two…. How are they different? Similar?

3. *Self-Expressive:* Imagine that you…. What could have caused this?

4. *Interpersonal:* Think about a time someone made you change your mind about…. How did they do it?

Assessment of students' responses to the hook provides valuable information as the teacher begins the lecture. This is DFA #1.

♦ *Step 5:* Determine how you will find out what students remember about the lecture.

New American Lecture Example

The New American Lecture is an updated view of a traditional and overused method of instruction. Because it is revised to allow time for students to think and reflect, teachers should stop *at least* every five minutes (shorten time based on level of students) to allow them time to interact with information.

♦ *Adjustment for struggling learners:* When teachers construct the New American Lecture for struggling learners they should design it based on students' instructional reading level, which is the level on which students will not be frustrated, but one at which they cannot read independently. Teachers might pause more often and use more whole-class discussion than with typical learners.

♦ *Adjustment for typical learners:* Teachers use the process of "Think-Pair-Share" (Lyman, 1981) to assess students' engagement in and understanding of the topic of the lecture.

♦ *Adjustment for gifted or highly advanced learners:* After modeling this process, teachers might ask gifted or highly advanced learners to work with a partner or in a small group to develop a New American Lecture that extends their understanding of a topic. Teachers may ask these students to present their New American Lecture to the class.

What follows is the "Assessment Target for New American Lecture Example: Graphing Linear Equations."

Assessment Target for New American Lecture Example: Graphing Linear Equations Curriculum

Curriculum
Standard: from the district or state
Essential Question: How do linear equations help us graph real-world problems?
Know: (Levels 1, 2, and 3) System of linear equations; how to collaborate. (Level 3) How to create and present a New American Lecture that applies understanding of graphing linear equations.
Understand that: Linear equations help us solve real-world math problems.

Assessment continues on next page.

Do: (Levels 1, 2, and 3) Reflect on information for the system of linear equations; graph data generated by linear equations; interact with the teacher's lecture; collaborate with a partner.
(Level 3) Create and present a New American Lecture applying ideas about linear equations.

Measurable Objective: (Levels 1, 2, and 3) Students will exemplify, generate, and classify in order to produce short written and spoken answers that accurately answer the questions prompted by the teacher's lecture about graphing linear equations.
(Levels 1, 2, and 3) Students will exemplify, classify, and generate in order to produce graphs that accurately reflect data from linear equations.
(Level 3) Students will exemplify, generate, classify, and create in order to produce a New American Lecture that is accurate and sufficient that applies their knowledge of how to graph linear equations.

Differentiation

Readiness: (Level 1) Present information that is on students' instructional reading level; pause more often; spend more time in whole-class discussion of information.
(Level 2) Think-Pair-Share (Lyman, 1981) helps to scaffold.
(Level 3) Create a New American Lecture with a partner or in small group.

Interests: Working with a partner and being able to interact with the teacher's instruction rather than passively listening can make learning more interesting.

Learning Styles: Mastery, interpersonal, understanding, and self-expression, mathematical/logical, analytical

Procedures (Levels 1 and 2)

♦ *Step 1:* Divide the material into chunks of information that should take five minutes or less to explain to students. For example, plan a lecture on "Solving Problems by Graphing Linear Equations."

♦ *Step 2:* Tell students that they are going to be participating in a new type of lecture, and that they should find a partner. If the number of students is uneven, allow three students to work together, but try to avoid more than one group of three.

How to find a partner in 3 steps:

1. Make eye contact with your partner.

2. Point to your partner.

3. Move to your partner without speaking.

♦ *Step 3:* After partnerships have formed, teachers activate students' interest in the topic by using this *hook*:

Think about where you have seen graphs used in the real world. Talk to your partner about your reactions to graphs. Do they help you understand things or do you ignore them?

(Notice that this question does not ask students to say what they know about solving systems by graphing because students may not know what those terms actually mean. It asks students to evaluate and verbalize a feeling about the topic.)

♦ *Step 4:* During this hook and for the rest of the lecture, teachers should use the process of "Think-Pair-Share" (Lyman, 1981). In other words, the teacher asks the students to think about their answer to this question for a few minutes (one minute may be sufficient). After students have had some time to think, the teacher prompts them either to write their ideas first and then share or to immediately share their ideas with their partner. After students have talked with their partners, allow time for them to share their answers with the whole class. (DFA #1)

♦ *Step 5:* Teachers may begin the lecture by handing out a sheet of paper with several two-column charts on the front and back. These charts will help students keep track of information about using linear equations to graph data. This presentation could be a PowerPoint or an explanation that includes interesting pictures, which teachers can easily find online and paste into the PowerPoint or other type of visual presentation. Present the lecture as follows:

- *Chunk 1:* Review the definition of a linear equation and show examples of how to use the two column chart to fill in data for the x-axis and y-axis. Students should use their sheet of charts to record what the teacher models. Teachers should base their examples on students' interests. For example, if many of the students in the class like sports, use a sports example to model the process.

- *Pause 1:* Turn to your partner and explain what you think is the hardest part of this process and which is the easiest. (Interpersonal—DFA #2)

- *Chunk 2:* Present another interesting example.

- *Pause 2:* Turn to your partner and take turns summarizing what you remember so far. (Mastery—DFA #3)

- *Chunk 3:* Hand out graph paper. Show students how to use the data from example 1 to graph the data.

- *Pause 2:* Turn to your partner and tell him or her how the data in the chart is similar to the data on the graph and also how it is different from that data. (Understanding—DFA #4)

- *Chunk 4:* Show students how to use the data from example 2 to graph the data.

- *Pause 4:* Turn to your partner and tell him or her how you might use this mathematical method to solve a problem in your life. (Self-Expressive—DFA #5)

- *Chunk 5:* Give students a problem that includes the equation and one part of the chart filled in. Work this problem with students. Then give them another problem that includes the equation and one part of the chart filled in.

- *Pause 5:* Collaborate with your partner to complete the chart. (Mastery—DFA #6)

- *Chunk 6:* Give students a real-world problem that includes a filled-in chart. In this part of the lecture, the teacher talks about how students might determine the equation from the information. See http://www.centerforcsri.org and click on "Webcasts" for interesting examples.

- *Pause 6:* Give students a series of questions about the filled-in chart, including which numbers would represent the y-axis, which would represent the x-axis, and what the equation would be. Ask them to answer the questions together. (Mastery—DFA #7)

♦ Continue presenting examples and pausing while partners practice. (DFA #8 and so on) When students are ready, the teacher administers a practice test of all of the various skills related to graphing linear equations (DFA number depends on how many times you have assessed). Teachers should give students who demonstrate mastery on this test enrichment problem to solve while they re-teach those who did not demonstrate mastery.

♦ This process continues until all students have demonstrated mastery in class or in after-school remediation.

Procedures (Level 3)

After you have quickly gone through the steps outlined for levels 1 and 2 above, allow students to work with the same partner or in a small group to create a similar New American Lecture that has the goal of demonstrating an application of graphing linear equations. Use the steps provided in this example to create a syllabus that outlines the steps and use Figure 3.9, "Rubric for Real-World Problem" (page 71), to evaluate this product.

♦ *Summative Assessment:* Can be a variety of assessment tasks, including multiple-choice or short-answer tests.

Direct Instruction

This strategy is an updated version of Madeline Hunter's *6-Step Lesson Plan* by Robin Hunter (2004). It allows for constant formative assessment during guided practice and independent practice.

Direct Instruction Example

♦ *Adjustment for struggling learners:* This lesson is leveled for typical learners; therefore, to adjust it for struggling learners, teachers may want to find a selection about pathogens that is on the learners' instructional reading level. Teachers may also want to ask the strongest students to act out the role play for the rest of the class.

♦ *Adjustment for typical learners:* For typical learners, the teacher should provide a script for the role-play activities so that the students do not have to make too many decisions about how to proceed. The process can allow for creativity, but not require them to create the form the role play will take.

♦ *Adjustment for gifted or highly advanced students:* This process can be adapted for gifted students by allowing them to choose how they will show how pathogens spread.

What follows is the "Assessment Target for Direct Instruction Example: Pathogens."

Assessment Target for Direct Instruction Example: Pathogens

Curriculum

Standard: from the district or state

Essential Question: How do pathogens spread?

Know: (Levels 1 and 2) How pathogens spread; how to collaborate on a role-playing activity.
(Level 3) How to choose and demonstrate a process.

Understand that: Knowing how pathogens spread can help us protect ourselves from getting sick from them.

Do: (Levels 1 and 2) Role play how pathogens spread.
(Level 3) Choose a method to demonstrate how pathogens spread; present to the class.

Measurable Objective: (Levels 1 and 2) Students will interpret, create, and execute in order to produce a role play that is thorough and accurate to demonstrate how pathogens spread.
(Level 3) Students will interpret, create, and execute in order to demonstrate in a thorough and accurate manner how pathogens spread.

Differentiation

Readiness: (Level 1) Choose instructional reading-level materials; strongest students act out the role play for the class.
(Level 2) Teacher-provided script does not require students to determine the form of the role play.
(Level 3) Allow students to choose a method for showing how pathogens spread.

Interests: Students get to choose their roles or their method of presentation.

Learning Styles: Interpersonal, kinesthetic, mastery, creative

Procedures (Levels 1 and 2)
Modeling

♦ *Step 1:* Have a whole-class conversation about what students already know about infectious diseases and get a sense of their interest in them. (DFA #1)

♦ *Step 2:* Model a lesson, such as understanding infectious diseases, using the following teaching methods:

• *Visual:* Show students pictures of bacteria, viruses, fungi, and protists that cause infectious diseases.

• *Oral:* Explain orally examples of each of these pathogens and how they are spread.

- *Kinesthetic:* Ask students to creatively act out passing a germ. For example use a symbol for a germ (a stuffed toy or a piece of paper) and start it into the classroom. Students demonstrate how the germ can make it around the room.

This part of the lesson may involve asking students to individually read a part of their textbook or another resource that also explains how we spread various pathogens.

Direct Practice

- ◆ *Step 3:* Divide the class into groups of six and assign these groups to show what they are learning by acting out "How Pathogens Spread: Role Play" (Figure 2.2). For struggling learners, teachers may ask one group of six to perform for the rest of the class. While the group is preparing, teachers might assign the rest of the class to read and take notes on a selection about pathogens.

  - *Materials needed:* Markers, string, glue, paper, sparkles, hats, and any costumes and props you might have. Creative teachers might have a "Role-Play Box" that they keep filled with these kinds of materials.

Give the assignment shown in Figure 2.2 to student groups.

Figure 2.2. How Pathogens Spread: Role Play

How Pathogens Spread

1. You are going to act out "How Pathogens Spread."

2. Take one of the following roles: bacterium, a virus, a fungus, protist, a human, a narrator. The narrator becomes the group leader and keeps the process moving.

3. Develop a costume for yourself that shows you know what the text says you might generally look like.

4. For each pathogen, write and practice speaking a description of yourself and how you might make a human sick. The person playing the human writes about and practices how pathogens make humans sick. The human must be able to act out getting sick in different ways. He/she must be able to vividly describe several illnesses, for example, African sleeping sickness. The narrator writes and practices presenting a summary of the events. The teacher circulates and acts as a guide on the side to troubleshoot and to make sure students are on the right track. (DFA #2)

5. When the role play begins, the narrator introduces each character (the bacterium, the virus, the fungus, the protist, and the human).

6. Each character describes himself or herself.

7. The human sits in a chair or stands and the narrator prompts each pathogen to act out and describe his/her attack on him/her.

8. The human acts out and describes his or her response to the pathogen.

9. The narrator makes a summary speech and all take a bow. (DFA #3)

Guided Practice

♦ *Step 4:* After the role play, the teacher might assign students to review what they have learned by rereading the text and writing questions or answering teacher made questions about it. Teacher's assess this work to determine if they should reteach any of the concepts. (DFA #4 and so on)

Summative assessment (independent practice) includes students taking a test (short answer, multiple choice, or other summative assessment) to show what they have learned.

Procedures (Level 3)

♦ Use Steps 1 and 2 from *Procedures (Levels and 2)*, page 35.

♦ *Step 3:* Divide the class into groups and pose this challenge:

Now that you know something about how pathogens spread, brainstorm with your group to choose a way to help us all remember how pathogens spread. Some suggestions are a role play or skit, a dance, a talk show, or a game show.

♦ *Step 4:* Give students time to develop their idea and time to present it to the class.

Summative assessment (independent practice) includes students taking a test (short answer, multiple choice, or other summative assessment) to show what they have learned.

Graduated Difficulty

The Graduated Difficulty strategy comes from the work of Mosston (1972) as adapted by Silver, Strong, and Perini (2007). It is a perfect strategy to use to assess math and science learning. Teachers should follow these steps to design a Graduated Difficulty strategy:

♦ *Step 1:* Choose knowledge or skill you want students to learn and create tasks for at least three levels of difficulty.

♦ *Step 2:* Create a means of evaluating student work (e.g., a rubric or a checklist).

♦ *Step 3:* Decide how you will present the tasks to students.

♦ *Step 4:* Help students preassess the tasks to determine at which level they can be successful.

♦ *Step 5:* Help students reflect about their work on the tasks.

Graduated Difficulty can also use ideas from "Gradual Release of Responsibility" (Wilhelm, Baker, & Dube, 2001) and Vygotsky's "Zone of Proximal Development." Figure 2.3 (page 38) is my interpretation of Vygotsky's (1986) "Zone of Proximal Development" combined with "Gradual Release of Responsibility" (Wilhelm et al., 2001).

Figure 2.3. Zone of Proximal Development Combined with Gradual Release of Responsibility

Teacher Controls	Students and Teachers Share Control	Student Controls
Teacher decides how and what students learn about a topic. Teacher instructs students.	**ZONE OF PROXIMAL DEVELOPMENT** Students do not reject the topic and are approximately developmentally ready to learn about it. Students are willing to *gradually accept responsibility for learning* about the topic.	Students are interested in the topic and ready to learn about it. Students independently learn about the topic.
Students observe and may or may not learn about the topic.	Teacher is aware of students' interests in the topic and their willingness to learn about it. Teacher uses strategies that challenge students to learn about the topic. Teacher *gradually releases responsibility for learning* about the topic to students.	Teacher observes students learning and may help if asked.

_____ Rigid boundary where it is hard for students and teachers to exchange ideas
_ _ _ _ Permeable boundary where students and teachers freely exchange ideas

Graduated Difficulty Example 1

♦ *Adjustment for struggling learners:* Teachers begin with easy processes and increase the difficulty as students demonstrate skills through formative assessments. For struggling learners, it is a good idea to minimize truly difficult problems. As much as possible, provide structuring for word problems because they are the most difficult. A graphic organizer like SOLVE (Enright, Mannhardt, & Baker, 2004) can help the teacher assess how well struggling learners are breaking down the problems in order to solve them.

What follows is the "Assessment Target for Graduated Difficulty Example: Word Problems."

Assessment Target for Graduated Difficulty Example: Word Problems

Curriculum
Standard: from the district or state
Essential Question: How can we use a graphic organizer to help us solve word problems in math?
Know: How to use a graphic organizer to solve increasingly complex word problems.
Understand that: Using a graphic organizer to "unpack" and organize math word problems make them easier to solve.
Do: Solve increasingly difficult math problems using a graphic organizer.
Measurable Objective: Students will classify and execute in order to produce work and solutions that are correct using a graphic organizer to address math word problems.

Differentiation
Readiness: (Level 1) Graduating the difficulty using a graphic organizer to structure and using gradual release of responsibility for solving the problems.
Interests: Teachers may find word problems, make them up, or teach students how to write word problems that address the real world.
Learning Styles: Mathematical/logical, mastery, analytical

Procedures

- *Step 1:* Model for students how to use the graphic organizer shown in Figure 2.4 (page 40) as they work math problems that become increasingly difficult, but not too difficult. Assess students' ability to use this graphic organizer using an easy sample problem. (DFA #1)

- *Step 2:* Present three different word problems: one that is easy, one that is somewhat harder, and one that is harder yet.

- *Step 3:* Students choose one of the three problems to solve using the graphic organizer. (DFA #2)

- *Step 4: Assess student performance on each problem.* Help students reflect on what was most difficult. Have similar word problems ready to present for more practice. (DFA #3, and so on)

Figure 2.4. Graphic Organizer for Solving a Word Problem in Math

Study the Problem ♦ Students could rewrite the problem here. ♦ Highlight the question (i.e., What is the problem asking me to find?).	
Organize the Facts ♦ List the facts. Cross out any unnecessary information.	
Line Up a Plan ♦ Decide what steps you need to take to solve the problem.	
Verify Your Plan with Action ♦ Put the numbers into your plan.	
Evaluate Your Answer ♦ Rewrite your answer in a complete sentence.	

Source: This is an adaptation of SOLVE by Enright et al. (2004).

Summative evaluation could include a test of students' ability to use the graphic organizer to solve a moderately difficult word problem. Teachers should encourage students to continue to use this organizer with increasingly difficult word problems throughout the year.

Graduated Difficulty Example 2

♦ *Adjustment for typical learners:* This is a perfect strategy to use to assess typical learners' math and science learning. The teacher begins with easy processes and increases the difficulty as students demonstrate skills through formative assessments. The teacher should expect typical learners to be able to master grade-level material and stretch toward more advanced levels. If teachers graduate difficulty for typical learners, they may not need too much scaffolding.

♦ *Adjustment for gifted or highly advanced learners:* For this example, which is leveled for typical learners, instead of telling students the data to collect, allow them to choose their own data. Teachers may want to allow students to brainstorm some categories, such as sports scores, daily temperatures, or weights of processed foods. Ask students to draw some conclusions about the patterns they notice from the data.

What follows is the "Assessment Target for Graduated Difficulty Example: Graphing Data." This is an integrated math–science example of graduated difficulty.

Assessment Target for Graduated Difficulty Example: Graphing Data (Math–Science Integration)

Curriculum
Standard: from the district or state
Essential Question: How can we create visual representations, like graphs, to show data?
Know: How to create various types of graphs of various kinds of data; reading graphs created from various data.
Understand that: Creating graphs helps us understand the meaning of various kinds of data.
Do: Create bar and line graphs and apply that learning to more difficult graphing problems.
Measurable Objective: (Level 2) Students will classify, organize, interpret, execute, and produce a bar graph and a line graph that are thorough and accurate reflections of collected data. (Level 3) Students will generate graphs that accurately reflect data from linear equations.

Differentiation
Readiness: (Level 2) Teacher-determined data; teacher-guided practice and reteaching if necessary. (Level 3) Student-determined data; students brainstorm ideas with teacher facilitation.
Interests: Using student data to create graphs motivates interest in the topic. Speaking about the topic in students' language also makes it more interesting.
Learning Styles: Mastery, interpersonal, understanding, and self-expression, mathematical/logical, analytical, kinesthetic, creative

Procedures

♦ *Step 1:* Activate learning by starting with a question typical learners will be able to answer. For example, "What is a graph?" The teacher may use "Think-Pair-Share" (Lyman, 1981), and then ask students to share with the whole class. This process allows the teacher to assess students' prior knowledge and interest in this topic. (DFA #1)

♦ *Step 2:* Present basic information about graphs in real-world (nontextbook) terms. For instance introduce the concept that a graph is a picture. Demonstrate a graph kinesthetically by having students come to the front of the room and line up according to their heights. The class could talk about the kind of picture this graph would be. Some may notice that this line up looks like a bar graph. The teacher should take as much time as needed to help students see graphs as nonthreatening scientific and mathematical concepts.

♦ *Step 3:* To determine if students understand the concept of graphing, the teacher should allow them to make a simple bar graph from collecting data in the classroom. This process should be fun and interesting to students. (DFA #2)

♦ *Step 4:* Give students the assignment shown in Figure 2.5.

Figure 2.5. Student Survey Graph Project

Student Survey Graph Project by_____

Part I

1. You may work with a partner or by yourself.

2. You need to find out the birth month of at least ten students in this class.

3. Make a chart that has each person's name and birth month beside it.

4. Interpret your data by noticing how many students were born in each month.

5. Make a bar graph that reflects your data.

After more instruction:

Part II

1. Use the same data to make a line graph.

2. Use the graph paper provided to write a title, draw your horizontal axis and vertical axis that has an origin of 0.

3. Label your horizontal and vertical axes to show your variables.

4. Use data points that accurately reflect your data.

5. Summarize your findings.

♦ *Step 4:* After students have completed Part I of their assignment (DFA #3), increase the difficulty to include instructing students about the definitions of terms such as horizontal axis, vertical axis, data points, axis labels, and origin.

♦ *Step 5:* Hand out graph paper and ask students to complete Part II of the "Student Survey Graphing Project." Move around the room to make sure students are responding appropriately to the assignment. (DFA #5) Collect these projects and evaluate them prior to moving on to more difficult processes, such as interpreting graphs made by others. (DFA #6)

♦ *Step 6:* Begin the process of teaching students to read line graphs made by others. After instruction and practice, assign students to answer questions about a specific line graph related to a science topic. (DFA #7)

Use a summative test to evaluate learning. If too many students do not show achievement, use the test as formative, and then reteach and retest.

Teams–Games–Tournaments

This strategy comes from the work of DeVries, Edwards, & Slavin (1978) as adapted by Silver, Strong, and Perini (2007). It is successful because, according to Silver et al. (2007), it:

- Is a great mixture of cooperation and competition.
- Is an effective cooperative learning activity.
- Uses repetition and variety to build knowledge on any topic.
- Provides excellent assessment data.
- Incorporates a scoring model that is motivational.
- Allows a variety of question types, for example, *six question types*, as follows:
  1. Similarities and differences questions
  2. Riddle questions (e.g., I am not a…, I am…. What am I?)
  3. Demonstrate a process (e.g., work a math problem)
  4. Develop an explanation (e.g., Give two reasons that….)
  5. Complete a pattern (e.g., What might be the next word: think, wink, sink,…?)
  6. Determine true or false

This strategy requires some work and planning up front, but allows teachers to function as troubleshooters once students learn how to play the games.

Teams–Games–Tournaments Example 1

- *Adjustment for struggling learners:* To use this strategy, teachers may feel they need to provide more structure for struggling learners. The following example is an adaptation that allows more teacher control.

What follows is the "Assessment Target for Teams–Games–Tournament Example: Water."

Assessment Target for Teams–Games–Tournament Example: Water

Curriculum
Standard: from the district or state
Essential Question: What is important to remember about water?
Know: How to answer various kinds of questions about water and work with a team.
Understand that: Water is critical to our existence and to preserve it, we need to understand and recall important information about it.
Do: Answer science questions about water.

Assessment continues on next page.

> **Measurable Objective:** Students will recall, generate, discriminate, and infer in order to produce oral responses that are correct about water.

Differentiation
Readiness: (Level 1) Original design adapted to allow for more teacher control.
Interests: Teamwork and competition is interesting for most students.
Learning Styles: Mathematical/logical, mastery, analytical, interpersonal, creative

Procedures (Level 1)

Take these steps to set it up:

♦ *Step 1:* Decide important ideas from this science unit on water and convert those ideas into approximately fifty questions using *six question types* (page 43) the ideas above for varied and interesting questions.

Here are some examples of questions teachers might use for this Science Example of Teams-Games-Tournaments:

• Similarities and differences questions

1. Name one way buoyant force and weight are similar. (*Answer:* They both have an effect on how an object floats and/or sinks in water.)

2. Name one way buoyant force and weight are different. (*Answer:* Buoyant force works against gravity and weight works with it.)

• Riddle questions

1. I make fog on windows and I change a gas to a liquid. What am I? (*Answer:* Condensation.)

2. I am sometimes above you. I form when water vapor cools, forms droplets, and attaches to dust. What am I? (*Answer:* A cloud.)

• Demonstrate a process

1. Explain what happens to molecules when water makes ice. (*Answer:* Molecules lose energy, move slowly, clump together, and form a rigid structure.)

2. Explain what happens to molecules when water makes steam. (*Answer:* Molecules move faster and spread out.)

• Develop an explanation

1. Name two reasons we should protect our wetlands. (*Answer:* They naturally filter water and they help control flooding because they absorb excess water when it rains heavily.)

2. Name two critically important reasons we should protect our water supplies. (*Answer:* We cannot live without safe water and many creatures use water as their habitats.)

- Complete a pattern

    1. Complete this pattern: Plants use water and sun to help them grow. These plants grow larger, and then…. (*Answer:* Animals use plants to help them grow.)

    2. Complete this pattern: Water on the ground evaporates into the air, condenses, and then…. (*Answer:* It rains bringing water back to the ground.)

- Determine true or false (Ask students to correct false answers.)

    1. Tributaries are not part of a river system. (*Answer:* False. They are part of the river system because they feed the river and are an important part of the system.)

    2. Three types of freshwater wetlands are bogs, swamps, and marshes. (*Answer:* True)

♦ *Step 2:* Divide the class into groups as follows: Each group should have one relatively high-functioning student, two middle-functioning students, and one low-functioning student. For this version of the Teams–Games–Tournament assessment, you may have more than four groups; generally, however, if there are more than four groups, it can get tricky. With struggling learners, it is best to have fewer, rather than more, students per group; therefore, if the class has an uneven number, make groups of three rather than of five or six.

♦ *Step 3:* Convert the questions created in Step 1 into a set of review cards for each table and make sure questions will not generate disagreement and controversy. Each table should also have an answer key.

♦ *Step 4:* Appoint a group leader (the highest functioning student), who will help the students take turns and check answers. Students practice answering the questions on the cards to prepare for the tournament. Teacher circulates to make sure students are on the right track and to correct misconceptions. (DFA #1)

♦ *Step 5:* The tournament can be the same day as the practice or the next day. For the tournament, take up the answer keys and cards. Make a score grid on the board and label it according to the number of groups participating.

♦ *Step 6:* Begin the tournament by explaining that you will ask the questions one at a time from the cards. Tell students that they can earn points for their group by correctly answering a question. Depending on the functioning level of the members of the class, call on groups one by one and individual students one by one to make sure all students have a chance to answer, or if you believe students will lose interest if the questions are rotated, make each question "free for all" to have a chance to answer. It is a good idea to keep some record of how individual students are doing so that you might group them for reteaching, enrichment, or after-school remediation. It also helps you determine whether the majority of the class is learning the material. At the end of the tournament, teachers can award points and grades. (DFA #2 for individuals and for class)

Teachers can use this method as scaffolding and then allow students to move to a more student-centered, student-responsible process represented in the example for typical learners that follows.

Teams–Games–Tournaments Example 2

♦ *Adjustment for typical learners:* Most typical learners can use this process as it was originally designed.

♦ *Adjustment for gifted or highly advanced learners:* Teachers should use the processes described in this example; however, they might adjust the process by teaching gifted or advanced learners to write the *six question types* for a science or math unit of study.

What follows is the "Assessment Target for Teams–Games–Tournaments Example: Perimeter and Area."

Assessment Target for Math Example of Teams–Games–Tournaments: Perimeter and Area

Curriculum
Standard: from the district or state
Essential Question: How can we calculate the perimeter and area for various geometric figures?
Know: How to calculate area and perimeter for various figures; how to work with a team to learn about area and perimeter.
Understand that: Calculating area and perimeter can help us solve real-world problems.
Do: Participate in a tournament to learn how to calculate area and perimeter for various geometric figures.
Measurable Objective: Students will recall, generate, and analyze so as to produce oral answers that are correct about the perimeter and area of various geometric shapes.

Differentiation
Readiness: (Level 2) Teacher-guided process. (Level 3) Ask students to write the questions for the tournament using the *six question types*.
Interests: Teamwork and competition are interesting for most students.
Learning Styles: Interpersonal, mastery, visual, tactual (pulling cards)

Procedures (Level 2)

♦ *Step 1:* Decide important ideas from the math unit on calculating perimeter and area of various geometric shapes and convert those ideas into approximately 50 questions using the *six question types* for varied and interesting questions.

Here are some examples of questions teachers might use for this math example of Teams–Games–Tournaments:

- Similarities and differences questions:
  1. How is finding the area of a shape similar to finding the perimeter? (*Answer:* They both have formulas and both use measurement.)
  2. How is finding the area of a shape different from finding the perimeter? (*Answer:* The formulas are different and the measures for area are in squared units.)
- Riddle questions
  1. You can find out my area by using ½ $h \times (a + b)$. I have a long side and a smaller side. What am I? (*Answer:* A trapezoid.)
  2. I am worth 3.14159…. I help you find the area of a circle. What am I? (*Answer:* Pi.)
- Demonstrate a process
  1. What is the area of a triangle that has a base length of 5 inches and a height of 4 inches? (*Answer:* 10 square inches)
  2. If you have a rectangular room that is 10 feet by 12 feet, what is the perimeter of a rug you might buy for it? (*Answer:* 44 feet)
- Develop an explanation
  1. If you want to find out if your bedroom furniture will fit in your new bedroom, which mathematics skills would you need? (*Answer:* You need to use both area and perimeter to figure out how much total space you have within the room and the length and width of the walls and furniture to find out if the walls are long enough and wide enough for the furniture.)
  2. Explain two real-world uses for finding the perimeter of a piece of land. (*Answer:* If you want to build a fence around it, you need to know how much material to buy. If you want to find out if you have room to a make an outdoor volleyball court, you have to know the plot of the land.)
- Complete a pattern
  1. Complete this pattern that represents the Pythagorean theorem: 3, 4, _____. (*Answer:* 5)
  2. Complete this information: A trapezoid with a perimeter of 27 has these sides: 3, 6, 6, and _____. (*Answer:* 12)

- Determine true or false (Ask students to correct false answers.)
    1. Pi is a finite number. (*Answer:* False. Pi is an infinite number that helps us find the approximate circumference of a circle.)
    2. The area of a shape is always expressed in square units. (*Answer:* True.)

♦ *Step 2:* Divide the class into groups as follows: Each group should have one relatively high-functioning student who is labeled "advanced," two or more middle-functioning students who are labeled "average," and one low-functioning student who is labeled "novice" or other innocuous designation. If teachers are uncomfortable with these designations, they should find designations more suitable to their classroom or school culture.

♦ *Step 3:* Make a set of review cards and a key for each table. Cards should only have the question on them; the key should have the answers.

♦ *Step 4:* Students elect a group leader who will help the students take turns and will check answers. If students need help to choose a leader, teach them this process:

Choosing a Leader

> Everyone in the group agrees that on the count of three everyone will point to the leader. Tell students they may point to themselves. If the group cannot efficiently choose a leader, the teacher should choose for them.

♦ *Step 5:* Students take turns answering the questions on the cards to prepare for the tournament. Students may take turns drawing cards, reading them, and answering them. The group leader will check the correctness of the answer. Circulate to make sure students are on the right track. (DFA #1)

♦ *Step 6:* The tournament can be the same day as the practice or the next day depending on the amount of class time available. Make sure each table has a set of cards and a key. All questions and keys should be the same; however, you may color code the cards to designate teams. The teams could choose their color in advance. They could also have a team name.

♦ *Step 7:* When it is time for the tournament to begin, give the signal that students designated "advanced" should go to the "advanced" table. Students designated "average" should go to one or more "average tables." The students designated "novice" should go to the "novice table."

♦ *Step 8:* Students elect a leader and proceed with the game as follows: Students take turns pulling a card from the stack of cards. The appointed or elected leader of the group checks to see that the student has answered the question correctly. This leadership role might rotate depending how often students play the game. Students earn points for their home group. Circulate to check students' progress. (DFA #2)

♦ *Step 9:* After each table has gone through all the cards or if time has run out, players return to their home teams to record and tally their total points. Teachers can award points and grades based on their classroom or school culture, and they can take a running total of team points in order to conduct a celebration that acknowledges teams' achievement at the end of the year. (DFA #3)

◆ *Formative Assessment:* It is a good idea to keep some record of how individual students are doing so that you might group them for reteaching, enrichment, or after-school remediation. It is also helps you determine if the majority of the class is learning the material. (This strategy is formative assessment of individual students as well as of the class performance level.) Students enjoy this process and the teacher gets a good idea of how much students are learning.

Procedures (Level 3)

◆ *Step 1:* Tell students they will need to write questions about perimeter and area in order to prepare for a game.

◆ *Step 2:* Hand out a copy of the *six question types* with at least one example that matches your unit for each one.

◆ *Step 3:* In a whole-class discussion, allow students to offer oral examples of question types about perimeter and area.

◆ *Step 4:* Invite students to work alone, with a partner, or in a small group (no more than four students) to generate five questions for each question type.

◆ *Step 5:* Collect the questions written by the students and create the Teams–Games–Tournament cards and keys. Then proceed with the process as explained in the procedures for Level 2.

Note: Struggling and typical learners may aspire to also write their own questions.

Summary

This chapter presents several examples of differentiated formative assessments using mastery-based strategies. Teachers can see from these examples that mastery-based strategies allow them to assess often to get a clear understanding of how students are achieving in terms of math and science topics. These formative assessment opportunities allow teachers to improve student mastery of concepts by adjusting instruction that might include regrouping students for differentiated remediation, enrichment, or reteaching.

3

Understanding-Based Differentiated Formative Assessments

This chapter provides leveled examples of embedding formative assessments into a specific differentiated instructional strategy called *understanding-based learning*. Understanding-based learning styles, according to Silver, Strong, and Perini (2007), focus on students' abilities to use the processes of reasoning, analyzing, and presenting evidence to learn and also to show what they have learned. Strategies that capture these abilities include compare and contrast, reading for meaning, concept attainment, and problem-based learning.

Compare and Contrast

According to Marzano, Pickering, and Pollock (2001), one of the most effective strategies for improving student achievement is asking students to identify similarities and differences. Teachers often use this strategy without properly preparing students to use it, and they also ask students to use it but then do not apply the information for a meaningful purpose. What follows are some suggested steps (adapted from Silver, Strong, & Perini, 2007) for conducting a lesson in which students compare and contrast.

- ◆ *Step 1:* Hook students' interest in the process of comparing and contrasting by asking them to compare and contrast interesting things from their lives (e.g., fast food restaurants, types of music). (DFA #1)

- ◆ *Step 2:* Choose two important concepts from a unit of study that you want students to compare.

- ◆ *Step 3:* Explain *why* it is important to compare and contrast these two concepts. This is an extremely important step that teachers often leave out.

- ◆ *Step 4:* For this first time, teachers should provide the criteria by which students should compare and contrast the two concepts. Criteria might be, for example, how the concepts are similar and different in terms of how they appear, how they function, and what they achieve.

- ◆ *Step 5:* Use a two-column organizer (Figure 3.1, page 54) to help students describe each of the concepts separately. (DFA #2)

- ◆ *Step 6:* Hand out a graphic organizer, such as a Venn Diagram (see Figure 1.1, page 5, for an example) or the one in Figure 3.2, page 55. Model for students the process of determining similarities and differences.

♦ *Step 7:* After you have completed the organizer discuss with students how this process has addressed the purpose you mentioned as you began. (DFA #3) Prompt students to answer questions like these:

- Are these two concepts more similar than they are different?

- In what ways are they similar? Different?

- What might cause them to be different? Similar?

- What is the most important similarity? Difference?

- Why is it important to know how these concepts are similar? Different?

- What conclusions can we draw from this comparison?

♦ *Formative Assessment:* As teachers model this process, they should keep track of whether students are catching on or not. They might use any number of informal checks for understanding as described in Waterman (2009). One example is asking students at strategic points during the modeling to privately rate their understanding. Teachers can do this by having students close their eyes and hold up one, two, or three fingers to designate level of understanding (Allen, 2007). This teacher modeling should prepare students to gradually take responsibility for comparing and contrasting on their own, and as they do so, teachers can use formative assessments to determine how they are doing so that they might regroup, reteach, remediate, or enrich. When teachers gradually release responsibility to students to use a compare-and-contrast graphic organizer, they might allow students to work with a partner or in a small group to use their textbooks or other sources to find ideas.

Compare and Contrast Example

♦ *Adjustment for struggling learners:* This example is leveled for typical learners; to make it more accessible for struggling learners teachers can do the following: provide the graphic organizer for students with the categories and at least one example already completed, read the information to students or use strong student readers, and work as a whole class to construct the summary sentence.

♦ *Adjustment for typical learners:* Typical learners should be able to easily follow this kind of process if the teacher models and checks for understanding along the way. Teachers can continue to complete the "criteria" part of the graphic organizer, and may want to include at least one example for each part of the organizer. Gradually, teachers should allow students to complete the organizer on their own; however, depending on the age and level of the class, students may continue to need some help determining criteria for comparing and contrasting.

♦ *Adjustment for gifted or highly advanced learners:* Assessing gifted or highly advanced learners' ability to compare and contrast information on math or science topics shows how well they can think at high levels, especially if the concepts they are comparing and contrasting are complex. Therefore, for this kind of assessment, it is not just the process, but the content and the purpose for comparing and contrasting that determines whether the assessment challenges or otherwise meets the needs of gifted or highly advanced students. The most appropriate summarizing activity for these students requires them to complete an extended writing product.

What follows are some suggested math and science topics that these students might compare and contrast:

Math Compare and Contrast Suggestions

- Give students a series of values related to a unit of study and ask them to determine if the values are equal, which is larger, or if it is possible to determine. (Similar to the Graduate Record Exam [GRE] method of assessing math understanding.)

- Compare and contrast mean, median, and mode in terms of their usefulness as measures of central tendency for various types of data.

- Make a chart that compares and contrasts the various types of equations in terms of math and science problems they help to solve.

Science Compare and Contrast Suggestions

- Compare and contrast the light and electron microscopes. Show your information through views you might see of the same objects through each microscope. Also explain why you might use one versus the other.

- Compare and contrast historical views of "the atom" in terms of our modern view. Choose points of comparison that include an evaluation of these views in terms of their creativity.

- Compare and contrast the life forms in freshwater and saltwater. Use pictures to show the differences and similarities.

What follows is the "Assessment Target for Compare and Contrast Example: Fractions and Decimals."

Assessment Target for Compare and Contrast
Example: Fractions and Decimals

Curriculum
Standard: from the district or state
Essential Question: How are fractions and decimals similar and different?
Know: Similarities and differences between fractions and decimals; how to compare and contrast.
Understand that: Knowing the similarities and differences between fractions and decimals helps us understand how they inform our decisions.
Do: Determine similarities and differences between fractions and decimals.
Measurable Objective: Students will compare and generate a graphic organizer that includes at least three differences and similarities between fractions and decimals.

Assessment continues on next page.

Differentiation
Readiness: (Level 1) Premade graphic organizer with examples filled in; read information as a class; construct summary as a class. (Level 2) Graphic organizer provided by the teacher, leveled for typical learners. (Level 3) Use the same process with more complex terms.
Interests: Teachers make this comparison important for real-world problem solving.
Learning Styles: Understanding, visual, investigative

Procedures

- *Step 1:* Introduce the process of comparing and contrasting by asking students to compare and contrast department stores that have different pricing scales, for example Walmart versus Neiman Marcus (or other pricey store with which your students are familiar). (DFA #1)

- *Step 2:* Tell students that you will be comparing and contrasting fractions and decimals so that they might understand how to apply this skill to shopping.

- *Step 3:* Tell students that you will compare fractions and decimals based on the following criteria: What do they look like? What do they represent? How are they used? How do they function?

- *Step 4:* Ask students to draw a two-column organizer on a piece of paper (or hand students one of these premade). As a class, describe fractions in terms of the criteria and list these criteria on one side of the diagram, and then do the same for decimals (Figure 3.1 provides an example). Make sure students are participating and clear up any misconceptions. (DFA #2)

Figure 3.1. Example of Two-Column Organizer Describing Fractions and Decimals

Fractions	Decimals
Look like (structure): *one number on top of another number (numerator and denominator)*	**Look like (structure):** *decimal point and whole number or several numbers, sometimes into infinity*
Represent: *part of a number*	**Represent:** *part of a number*
Used: *to designate a ratio and proportion*	**Used:** *to figure percentages*
Function: *as a way to divide or to show divisions and relationships between numbers*	**Function:** *as a way to show how close a number is to 1*

◆ *Step 5:* Help students complete the "Similarities and Differences Graphic Organizer" (Figure 3.2). The "Criteria" part should be completed by the teacher. The class might work as a group to complete the rest of the organizer. (DFA #3)

◆ *Formative Assessment:* Use informal checks for understanding based on students' participation in the whole class activity. Teachers might ask students to complete the "Summary" part of the organizer as a formative assessment. (DFA #4)

Figure 3.2. Similarities and Differences Graphic Organizer

Alike?		
Fractions		**Decimals**
Are less than 1		
Can represent the same value		
Have symbols that identify them		
Can be used to help consumers understand the value of sales items		
Different?		
Fractions	**Criteria**	**Decimals**
Has one number on top (numerator) and another underneath (denominator)	**Structure**	Has decimal that is followed by one or more numbers
A ratio and proportion	**Represent**	A part of 10
To show the relationship between two numbers that are part of a whole	**Use**	To show parts of a number by 10s, 100s, etc.
To show ratios and proportions	**Function**	To show how close a number is to 1
Summarize: It is important to be able to determine the effect of a fraction and a decimal on a specific amount and then compare those results. When we shop, it might help us to understand how retailers advertise sale items. If we understand the differences and similarities between fractions and decimals, we might better understand how to determine which deals are better. For example, which is a better deal, one-third off or a 30% discount?		

Source: This similarities and differences graphic organizer is adapted from Drs. Max and Julia Thompson's *Learning Focused Strategies Notebook Teachers Materials.* Teachers can find wonderful resources for all kinds of learning focused graphic organizers by visiting http://www.manatee.k12.fl.us/sites/highschool/bayshore/Documents/L-F_Graphic_Organizers%202.pdf (retrieved October 12, 2009).

Summative assessment could include evaluating students' ability to apply the concepts as they appear in mathematics problems or in a science reading selections.

Reading for Meaning

To formatively assess student learning, it is critical that teachers assess students' ability to comprehend the primary textbook and other reading materials they use in the classroom. It is clear that if students cannot access the primary reading materials, teachers have two choices: (a) find alternative reading materials, or (b) provide scaffolding of that material. For math, teachers are looking not only for word literacy but also for number (or mathematics) literacy. Because numbers are abstract, teachers must realize that some students, especially in early middle school, may struggle to make sense of numbers and to be able to manipulate them to solve problems. Mathematics teachers often complain that students seem to "get it" during class, but "forget it" for the test. Assessing students often and revisiting important mathematics skills is critical for reading math for meaning. For science, teachers should assess students' ability to apply unfamiliar science vocabulary to real world experiences. Science terms are some of the most difficult to comprehend; therefore, teachers must not assume that examining new words a few times will make them memorable for many students. Also science and mathematics' texts have a certain grammar that can make them difficult to comprehend. Teachers can help students better understand these kinds of texts by taking some time to point out their structure.

These strategies, which are based on the work of Herber (1970) as adapted by Silver, Strong, and Perini (2007), include assessing students' abilities to demonstrate reading and mathematics comprehension. According to Herber (1970) and Silver, Strong, and Perini (2007), there are ten kinds of statements aligned with basic reading comprehension categories that might serve to inspire students to find answers as they read a text. These statements are proposed as a prereading activity to pique students' interests in the selection. This strategy is similar to an "Anticipation Guide," but it differs in that its goal is to strategically address reading comprehension skills. I have adapted their list of statement types as follows:

1. Vocabulary

2. Main idea

3. Inference

4. Details that build a case

5. Visualizing

6. Connections (text to text, text to world, text to self)

7. Symbols and metaphors

8. Writer's style

9. Empathizing

10. Personal perspective

The basic idea with this strategy is that teachers write statements based on the above ten categories. They ask students to agree or disagree with each statement, and then read to find out if they were right or wrong. Teachers might develop a graphic organizer (see Figure 3.4, page 59) to help them formatively assess students based on how well they address these statements. They may ask students to write "Proof" of their agreement or disagreement with the statement.

Reading for Meaning Example

♦ *Adjustment for struggling learners:* This formative assessment strategy is extremely important for struggling learners, who often have difficulty reading. To adjust this example, which is leveled for typical learners, teachers should find materials that explain photosynthesis and respiration at the instructional reading level of the majority of the class. If reading levels vary too widely, teachers may want to use cluster grouping in order to allow students to read selections matched more closely with their instructional reading level.

♦ *Adjustment for typical learners:* Reading for meaning requires that students have a working understanding of the important vocabulary of the discipline. There are many vocabulary assessment strategies; however, one of the best formative assessment strategies requires that students fully explain words. It is important that the science teacher help students understand that science terms are like any other vocabulary term that has a definition and an application. For typical learners, it is important to constantly assess science vocabulary terms so that students will have a greater likelihood of remembering them as they go on to their next level of education, be it high school or college.

♦ *Adjusted for gifted or advanced learners:* Ask these students to demonstrate reading comprehension through the process of completing an inquiry-based project or research report on this topic. By assigning these students to inquire further about the topic, they must critically read information on various levels and must synthesize the information.

What follows is the "Assessment Target for Reading for Meaning Example: Photosynthesis and Respiration."

Assessment Target for Reading for Meaning Example: Photosynthesis and Respiration

Curriculum
Standard: from the district or state
Essential Question: What are the causes and effects of photosynthesis and respiration?
Know: The causes and effects of photosynthesis and respiration.
Understand that: Photosynthesis and respiration are important processes for the health and growth of plants.
Do: (Level 1) Use instructional reading level materials about photosynthesis and respiration. (Level 2) List the causes and effects of photosynthesis and respiration. (Level 3) Write an inquiry-based report on photosynthesis and respiration.

Assessment continues on next page.

Measurable Objective: (Levels 1 and 2) Students will interpret, generate, infer, classify, and attribute information in a cause-and-effect graphic organizer that is accurate about photosynthesis and respiration.
(Level 3) Students will interpret, generate, infer, classify, and create an inquiry-based report that is accurate and sufficient about photosynthesis and respiration.

Differentiation

Readiness: (Level 1) Teachers use materials that match students' instructional reading levels.
(Level 2) Graphic organizer provided by the teacher.
(Level 3) Students write an inquiry-based report.

Interests: (Levels 1 and 2) Having blanks to fill is interesting to most learners.
(Level 3) Students enjoy finding information online.

Learning Styles: Understanding, visualization, investigative

What follows is an example of a science assessment that allows the teacher to assess the students' ability to read for meaning. It requires students to understand cause and effect related to critical science vocabulary terms.

Procedures (Levels 1 and 2)

♦ *Step 1:* Hand out a selection on photosynthesis and respiration.

♦ *Step 2:* Hand out the graphic organizer shown in Figure 3.3. Figure 3.4 is the key to the graphic organizer. Note that the best way to make these is to make the key and then take away information on one side or the other.

Figure 3.3. Identifying Causes and Effects in Photosynthesis and Respiration

Cause	Effect
1. The sun's light	1. Plants get energy that allows plants to make their own food.
2.	2. Chloroplasts in plant cells capture energy.
3.	3. Makes plants green
4. Photosynthesis	4.
5. Carbon dioxide + water	5.
6.	6. Cells break down simple food molecules and release their energy.
7. Sugar + Oxygen	7.

8.	8. Provides energy to cells without needing oxygen.
9.	9. Releases a small amount of energy
10. In the cells mitochondria, the smaller molecules combine with oxygen to produce water and carbon dioxide.	10.

Figure 3.4. Identifying Causes and Effects in Photosynthesis and Respiration (Key)

Cause	Effect
1. The sun's light	1. Plants get energy that allows plants to make their own food.
2. Sunlight	2. Chloroplasts in plant cells capture energy.
3. Chlorophyll	3. Makes plants green
4. Photosynthesis	4. The production of oxygen
5. Carbon dioxide + water	5. Sugar + oxygen
6. Respiration	6. Cells break down simple food molecules and release their energy.
7. Sugar + Oxygen	7. Carbon dioxide + water + energy
8. Fermentation	8. Provides energy to cells without needing oxygen.
9. In the cytoplasm, glucose is broken down into smaller molecules	9. Releases a small amount of energy
10. In the cells mitochondria, the smaller molecules combine with oxygen to produce water and carbon dioxide	10. Releases a large amount of energy

♦ *Step 3:* Begin reading the selection as a class. Model how to use the graphic organizer. Do examples with students until they seem comfortable with the process. (*Note:* Struggling learners may need the teacher to complete the entire graphic organizer with them for their first experience with it.)

Formative assessment is collecting the graphic organizer to make sure students understand photosynthesis and respiration. (DFA #1) If students show any faulty ideas or misunderstandings, teachers may address them in order to regroup, reteach, remediate, or enrich.

Summative assessment could be multiple choice, short answer, extended writing assignment, project regarding photosynthesis and respiration, or use the steps outlined in *Procedures (Level 3).*

Procedures (Level 3)

- *Step 1:* Ask students to use the Procedures for Level 2 to complete the graphic organizer (Figure 3.3, page 58) independently, with a partner, or in a small group.

- *Step 2:* Ask students to extend their understanding and knowledge of photosynthesis and respiration by completing an inquiry-based report. (See Figure 6.16, page 126, for a research paper holistic rubric.) Ask students to use the "Big Six" process (see Chapter 5, "Jigsaw," page 99, for resources) to complete a 500-word inquiry-based research report on photosynthesis and respiration or you may allow them to show their knowledge and understanding through an artistic project.

Concept Attainment

This strategy includes assessing students' abilities to explore in depth what complex words might mean. I find the methods from Frayer, Frederick, and Klausmeir (1969), Taba (1962), and Bruner (1973) most useful for differentiating formative assessment. Teachers adjust the level of learning not by adjusting these processes, but by adjusting the concepts they help to explore.

- *Adjustment for struggling learners:* Explore the concept *disease* and the math facts that equal 12 (presented here).

- *Adjustment for typical learners:* Explore the concept on typical learners' instructional reading level. Suggested example: equations.

- *Adjustment for gifted or highly advanced learners:* Explore the concepts on gifted or highly advanced learners' reading level. Suggested example: correlation and/or regression.

What follows is the "Assessment Target for Concept Attainment Examples Using Frayer et al. (1969), Taba (1962) and Bruner (1973) Models: Disease." All examples are leveled for struggling learners.

Assessment Target for Concept Attainment Example
Using the Frayer and the Taba Models: Disease

Curriculum
Standard: from the district or state
Essential Question: What is a disease?
Know: The concept of disease, how to categorize.
Understand that: Disease is a pathological condition of a part, organ, or system of an organism resulting from various causes, such as infection, genetic defect, or environmental stress, and characterized by an identifiable group of symptoms.
Do: Brainstorm, group concepts, categorize, draw conclusions.

Measurable Objective: Students will generate, classify, compare, and organize a list of words that define in detail and complexity the concept of disease.
Differentiation
Readiness: (Level 1) Teacher-led whole-class process with concepts at instructional level for struggling learners. (Level 2) Same process but use concepts on typical learners' instructional reading level. (Level 3) Same process but use concepts on gifted or highly advanced learners' instructional level.
Interests: Brainstorming and grouping allows students to actively participate in the process.
Learning Styles: Understanding, visual, investigative

Frayer's Model of Concept Development Example

Frayer et al. (1969) suggest that students might learn new concepts by asking them to discover the relational aspects of words. The four categories include the concept's definition, characteristics, examples and nonexamples.

Frayer Procedures

♦ *Step 1:* Identify a critical word that is complex and that students need to know in order to be successful in the unit. (DFA #1—whole class) (This process of identification could be the first formative assessment, if teachers determine whether or not students have misconceptions about the term.) The concept for this example is "disease."

♦ *Step 2:* Present students with the Frayer Model Graphic Organizer (Figure 3.5, page 62) and ask them to work on their own or with a partner to complete it. (DFA #2)

♦ *Step 3:* Have an overhead, white board, or LCD to show the Frayer Model Graphic Organizer so that the whole class may complete it together. (DFA #3—whole class)

♦ *Step 4:* Teachers may ask students to individually complete another "Frayer Model Graphic Organizer" for another complex term during the next class. (DFA #4)

Figure 3.5. Frayer Model Graphic Organizer: Disease

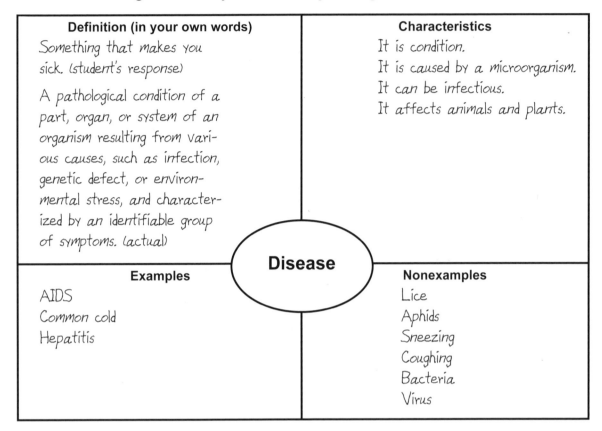

Definition (in your own words)	Characteristics
Something that makes you sick. (student's response) A pathological condition of a part, organ, or system of an organism resulting from various causes, such as infection, genetic defect, or environmental stress, and characterized by an identifiable group of symptoms. (actual)	It is condition. It is caused by a microorganism. It can be infectious. It affects animals and plants.
Examples AIDS Common cold Hepatitis	**Nonexamples** Lice Aphids Sneezing Coughing Bacteria Virus

(center oval: **Disease**)

Hilda Taba's Model of Concept Development Example

According to Hilda Taba (1962), students might significantly improve their abilities to reason and think abstractly if the teacher gives them chances to practice developing complex concepts. What follows is an example of a Taba concept development lesson.

Taba Procedures

♦ *Step 1:* Decide what concept to explore in depth with students. (DFA #1—whole class) The teacher should use two criteria for determining the concept to develop: (a) The concept must be highly important to the unit of study, and (b) it should be a concept that is multifaceted and possibly hard to fully understand.

♦ *Step 2:* Put the concept on the board and ask students to brainstorm an exhaustive list of words that they relate to the concept. The teacher records their responses. (DFA #2)

♦ *Step 3:* Students take turns choosing terms to group by two. The students must state how the terms are alike using this stem "_____ and _____ are alike because they both...." For example, "fever" and "rash" are alike because they are both "symptoms of a disease." Students may be tempted to say how the terms *relate* to one another, such as "_____ is part of _____"; however, they must be prompted not to group terms by two for that reason. For example, students might be tempted to group "fever" with "cold" because "fever" is a *symptom* of a "cold," but this is not the way to group. The teacher should correct any incorrect grouping suggestion. As students group by two, they should give each term a label. For example, "fever" is like "rash" because they are both "symptoms." The label would be "symptoms." Students may use words to combine more than once.

♦ *Step 4:* After students have combined all or most of the terms and labeled them, they should collapse categories and subsume lesser ideas under overarching ones. After you have completed this process, dispose of what the students have listed *and begin the same process over again.* The rationale for doing this is that students' thinking deepens when they repeat the process.

A Taba lesson can help the teacher and students assess their knowledge of concepts that are essential to their understanding of a core topic. (DFA #3)

Here is a list of some math and science concepts a teacher might use to explore in a Taba Concept Development Lesson:

♦ *Math:* algorithm, variables, translations, rational expressions, arithmetic, algebra, inequalities, ratio, proportion, measurement, probability, geometry, sequence, polynomial, slope

♦ *Science:* biotechnology, chemistry, biology, geology, matter, energy, disease, health, experiment, physics, electricity, biochemistry, laboratory, hypothesis

Figure 3.6 is the Taba Model in Chart Form for the science concept *disease.*

Figure 3.6. Taba Model in Chart Form

Concept to Explore: Disease
Brainstorm words that are related to disease: sickness, discomfort, bacteria, virus, doctors, fever, rash, medicine, hospitals, prescriptions, diagnosis, chicken soup, Jell-O, death, coughing, sneezing, tissues, sore throat, cancer, tumors, headaches
Put words in pairs and say how they are alike: Chicken soup and Jell-O are alike because they are both foods people eat when they have a disease. Sore throat and fever are alike because they are both symptoms people get when they have a disease. Bacteria and viruses are alike because they are both causes of disease. Medicines and prescriptions are alike because they are both treatments for disease. Medicines and rest are alike because they are ways to cure diseases.

Figure continues on next page.

Label pairs:
Chicken soup and Jell-O—foods Sore throat and fever—symptoms Bacteria and viruses—causes Medicines and prescriptions—treatments Medicine and rest—ways of curing

Subsume some categories under others:
I. Ways of Curing
    A. Treatments
    B. Foods
II. Symptoms
    A. Causes

Start over.
Draw conclusions that reflect deep learning about the concepts.

Jerome Bruner's Model of Concept Development Example

Teachers could also use Bruner's model to explore "disease"; however, I decided to present an example using a mathematics topic. Struggling learners might learn a great deal about complex concepts using Jerome Bruner's (1973) process of "Concept Attainment." What follows is the "Assessment Target for Concept Attainment Example from Bruner: Math Facts that Equal 12."

Assessment Target for Concept Attainment from Bruner: Math Facts that Equal 12

Curriculum
Standard: from the district or state
Essential Question: What are math facts that equal the number 12? (Do not share this essential question with students because part of the strategy is for students to guess this essential idea.)
Know: Math facts that equal 12, how to learn a math concept using Bruner's concept attainment.
Understand that: We can deepen our understanding of the number 12 by grouping and categorizing ideas about it. (Also, do not share with students until end of lesson.)
Do: Use the process of concept attainment to learn math facts that equal 12.
Measurable Objective: Students will generate, classify, compare, and organize a list of numbers that define in detail and complexity math facts that equal 12.

Differentiation
Readiness: (Level 1) Teacher-led whole-class process.
Interests: Suspense and guessing create interest.
Learning Styles: Understanding, visual, investigative

Procedures

The information and examples for this assessment strategy were adapted from this website: http://www.csus.edu/indiv/p/pfeiferj/EdTe226/concept%20attainment/ca_form.doc (retrieved April 12, 2008).

♦ *Step 1:* Select a math concept, such as "math facts that equal 12." Next determine attributes that would fit under the "no" and the "yes" column. Make cards that are large enough for the students to see with one of the attributes listed on each card. Cards for this example would look like this and have tape on the backs so that the teacher can attach them to the chart:

$$7 + 5$$

- Positive examples are: $7 + 5$, 2×6, $6 + 6$, $10 + 2$, 3×4, $14 - 2$
- Negative examples are: $10 - 1$, 5×2, $6 - 6$, $10 - 2$, 4×2, $14 - 0$

♦ *Step 2:* Hand out the following worksheet shown in Figure 3.7 so that students might record what is happening on the board.

Figure 3.7. Student Worksheet

Concept Attainment

Student Worksheet   Student's Name: _____

Yes	No

- *Step 3:* Show the cards one at a time to the students. For the first card, 7 + 5, say, "This card is a 'Yes.'" For the next card, which could be 10 − 1, say "This card is a 'No.'" Repeat this process until there are three examples on the board. (DFA #1)

- *Step 4:* Ask students to look at the "Yes" column and ask what the numbers have in common. Tell students not to say out loud what they notice. (DFA #2)

- *Step 5:* Hold up the next three cards and ask students to say in which column they should go. Some students will get it and others may not. Ask students to offer more examples, and prompt them to reveal the concept, which is "Math facts that equal 12." (DFA #3) If one or more students never understand, teachers might reteach them or remediate them.

- *Step 6:* Facilitate a discussion among students so that they may evaluate the process and talk about how they might apply it to future concept attainment activities. (DFA #4)

A summative assessment for any of these three models can include students generating an accurate definition of the concept or choosing it in a multiple-choice test. Also teachers might evaluate students' ability to use the concept as it appears in the context of unit objectives. In other words, summative assessment for concept attainment will include determining if students can successfully use the concept.

Problem-Based Learning

Inquiry-based learning is based on the work of Suchman (1966). According to Marzano, Pickering, and Pollock (2001), there are at least six problem-based models: Problem Solving, Decision Making, Systems Analysis, Historical Investigation, Invention, and Experimental Inquiry. Silver, Strong, and Perini (2007) add a seventh model called Mystery. For this strategy all three readiness levels might follow the same process to explore their various interests.

Real-World Problem Solving Example

- *Adjustment for struggling learners:* This strategy is an excellent way to formatively assess struggling learners' learning. As Sagor and Cox (2004) stated, struggling learners (they refer to these students as at-risk students) need to believe that what they are learning is worthwhile; consequently, this kind of assessment can be highly effective for them. Knowing the interests of struggling learners is critical for planning this kind of assessment; therefore, the topic must motivate students to work to solve it. What follows are some math and science topics that might interest struggling learners. Teachers may want to survey them early in the year to find out exactly what might interest them.

- *Math:* making money, getting good deals (consumerism) on items they might buy like clothes, recreational activities, music, technologies, measuring for decorating their personal space, problem solving in art, issues that deal with splitting things with friends, cooking, and sports statistics.

- *Science:* sexually transmitted diseases and biological functions related to sexuality, environmental issues, health issues that specifically affect them, heredity, careers in science.

♦ *Adjustment for typical learners:* This strategy is an excellent way to formatively assess typical learners' because it shows how an academic topic applies to the real world. Typical learners should enjoy a chance to participate in a real-world problem solving assessment process, but teachers must not make it too open-ended. Therefore, they could offer problem choices and give students specific guidelines for solving one of them. The lesson presented here is structured for typical learners.

♦ *Adjustment for gifted or highly advanced learners:* This strategy is an excellent way to formatively assess gifted or highly advanced learners. Using problem-based learning strategies fits these students very well. What follows is a list of sources for real-world math or science problems.

Websites (all retrieved April 12, 2008):

- www.udel.edu/pbl

   This website includes several high-level problems including those for chemistry and physics.

- http://www.cotf.edu/ete/modules/modules.html

   This website has basic, comprehension, and advanced problems.

- http://www.fpspi.org/topics.html

   This is the site for Future Problem Solvers International. It includes several practice problems as well as released topics from 2006–07 and 2007–08.

Here are some good books for real-world science and math problems:

- *Thinking Toward Solutions: Problem Based Learning Activities for General Biology* by Eldra Solomon, Linda Berg, and Diana Martin (Solomon, Berg, & Cole, 1998)

   This book may be a good source of problems for science teachers.

- *Mathabililty: Math in the Real World* by Michael Cain (Cain, 2005)

   The problems in this book are presented in four formats: step-by-step, prompted practice, independent practice, and challenge. On each page, the author presents a real-world problem that requires a variety of math skills (noted under the title). For example the problem called "Moving Belts and Improving Belts" covers the Pythagorean formula and multistep problem solving. There is space to work problems, so this book is basically a workbook.

- *Real Life Math Mysteries: The Kids' Answer to the Question, "What Will We Ever Use This For?"* by Maya Washington Tyler (Tyler, 2005)

  The title is somewhat misleading. In this book, the author identifies real people who use math in their work. She includes a picture of them and their signatures to make them seem real. She includes their testimonials about how they felt about math when they were in school, which was often negative, and how they need math skills to perform their current jobs. For each of the jobs, including banker, landscaper, archeologist, nurse, and twenty-seven others, the author includes a challenging problem involving a variety of math skills.

- *25 Real Life Math Investigations that will Astound Teachers and Students* by Edward and Luke Zaccaro (Zaccaro & Zaccaro, 2007)

  This book has astounding math problems and lots of cute pictures of a character that looks like Einstein and other goofy characters. Even though the math problems are challenging and interesting, the format might appeal to elementary students more than to middle or high school students. Some of the chapters provide excellent consumer advice, such as "How People Lie with Statistics" and "Be Careful when you 'Rent to Own.'"

- *Extreme Math* by Kip Tyler and Marya Washington Tyler (Tyler & Tyler, 2003)

  Each chapter describes the extreme activities of ten or so people. The authors set up the situation and then ask several computations questions about various aspects of it. For example, in the chapter about Jeff Gildehau, a hang glider, the computation questions ask students to prepare a chart comparing statistics on two hang gliders and some questions about how long they could stay in the air given certain situations.

What follows is the "Assessment Target for Real World Problem Example: Chemical Reactions."

Assessment Target for Real World Problem Example: Chemical Reactions

Curriculum
Standard: from the district or state
Essential Question: How can we solve a real-world problem involving chemical reactions?
Know: How to research a science topic in order to solve a real problem; how to construct a product (such as brochure, PowerPoint, or booklet) to show how to solve the problem; more information about the topic related to the problem.
Understand that: Chemical reactions can cause real world problems that we can solve.

Do: Research, create a booklet, PowerPoint, or brochure to help solve a problem.

Measurable Objective: Students will generate, plan, produce, create, implement, organize, and evaluate a solution that is an efficient, effective, and creative way to address chemical reactions in the real world.

Differentiation

Readiness: (Level 1) Teachers and/or students choose a high-interest problem. (Level 2) Teacher uses checkpoints to assure students are proceeding as they should. (Level 3) Teachers and/or students choose a more complex problem.

Interests: Students choose from a list of projects.

Learning Styles: Understanding, creative, investigative

Procedures

◆ *Step 1:* Present the syllabus (Figure 3.8, page 70) to students and allow them time to choose one of the problems. Their choice is DFA #1. Use the rubric shown in Figure 3.9 (page 71) to evaluate solutions.

◆ *Step 2:* Allow students to find sources of information in the school media center or as a homework assignment. Checking that students have selected appropriate sources of information to solve their problems is DFA #2.

◆ *Step 3:* Give students time to take notes for their products. Checking the notes students take to complete the product is DFA #3.

Figure 3.8. Syllabus for Solving a Real-World Science Problem: Chemical Reactions

◆ *Step 1:* Choose a problem from the ones listed below related to the unit on "Chemical Reactions." Or propose another problem and get the teacher's permission to work on it instead.

> ◆ *Problem 1:* Older people, children, and some sensitive adults are susceptible to the chemicals found in our buildings, in the atmosphere, and in our water supply. Find out which chemicals are most dangerous to these people and make a brochure, Power-Point, or booklet that might help them.

> ◆ *Problem 2:* Every year fire destroys homes and kills people. Students learn fire safety as soon as they get to school, but we continue to have loss of property and loss of lives because people do not understand fire. Make a brochure, PowerPoint, or booklet that you might show to a group of elementary students and their parents about fire and fire safety.

> ◆ *Problem 3:* American teenagers are hooked on fast foods, but although these foods taste good, they contain unhealthy substances. Find out how the chemicals in fast foods affect those who eat them and design a brochure, PowerPoint, or booklet to explain how dangerous they can be to the health of those who eat them.

◆ *Step 2:* Find at least three sources of information to inform your work. Make sure to cite these sources in MLA form.

◆ *Step 3:* What follows are the dates parts of the project are due:

> ◆ Your decision about the problem you will address and where you plan to find information
> Date Due: _____

> ◆ Notes you have taken on the topic
> Date Due: _____

> ◆ Plan for the product
> Date Due: _____

> ◆ Product
> Date Due: _____

Figure 3.9. Rubric for Real-World Problem

Criteria	Level 1	Level 2	Level 3	Level 4
Content	The amount of information included in the product does not sufficiently cover the topic and/or many of the facts are inaccurate.	The amount of information included in the product leaves out many important ideas and/or includes some ideas that are inaccurate.	The product includes enough ideas to adequately cover the topic and all ideas are accurate.	The product includes in-depth and accurate information that exceeds the expectations for the product.
Organization	The information in the product appears to be arranged in a random manner.	The information in the product is arranged so that it is hard to follow and confusing.	The information in the product is well-organized and easy to follow.	The organization of the product matches exceptionally well with the information.
Style	The information is basic and uninteresting. It contains many errors and is sloppy.	The information, which is mostly well-known, contains some errors. No depth.	The information contains no major errors and the writer includes some interesting and important ideas.	The information contains no major errors. The writing style includes interesting uses of language and important facts.
Originality	The information is taken directly from a source with no attempt to synthesize it.	The information is not presented in a way that differs much from the sources from which it was taken.	The product is creative and interesting and shows a synthesis of the information.	The product is very interesting and shows an exceptionally creative solution to the problem.

Note: For typical learners, the problem assessment should not be too open-ended, teachers should require checkpoints to make sure students are proceeding as they should, and the rubric is written in terms that students should be able to understand. Teachers should make sure students understand it by asking them to paraphrase it either orally or in writing.

♦ *Step 4:* Allow students time in class to create a plan for their product. Provide ongoing checks for appropriateness. Checking the plan for the product is DFA #4.

♦ *Step 5:* Allow students to present their products to the class. Allowing this presentation and the product represent DFA #5.

Summative assessment might include a multiple-choice test, short-answer test, or extended writing assignment on chemical reactions.

Summary

This chapter presents several examples of strategies that address understanding-based learning and assessment. Students who prefer this learning style are curious and motivated to use reason, logic, and evidence to solve problems. These strategies offer many opportunities to formatively assess student learning that prepares them to achieve on summative measures that are similar. Notice the large number of thinking verbs that students need for solving real-world problems. The next chapter provides examples of self-expressive formative assessments.

4

Self-Expressive–Based Differentiated Formative Assessments

This chapter provides leveled examples of embedding formative assessments into a specific differentiated instructional strategy called self-expressive–based learning. According to Silver, Strong, and Perini (2007), self-expressive learning strategies focus on imagination and creativity. Students who learn best through this style have strong needs to express their individuality and originality. Silver et al. (2007) divide this style into four main types: inductive learning, metaphorical expression, pattern maker, and mind's eye.

Inductive Learning

Silver, Strong, and Perini (2007) suggest using this method either to introduce a unit or to review for a unit. Using inductive learning is also an excellent way to formatively assess student learning about the key elements in a unit of study. This is a brainstorming and predicting process that includes grouping, labeling, and generalizing to construct essential ideas. It is a wonderful assessment strategy to use if teachers want learners to truly understand challenging or essential concepts.

Inductive Learning Example

This inductive learning example demonstrates how teachers might use the same learning process with differing student interests. In other words, all students are using inductive reasoning, but with different content.

- *Adjustment for struggling learners:* Graphic organizers that promote inductive learning help struggling learners deepen their understanding of inequalities.

- *Adjusted for typical learners:* These learners use a somewhat more complicated graphic organizer to facilitate inductive learning about contour maps.

- *Adjustment for gifted or highly advanced learning:* These learners may enjoy a topic that combines use of technology with the process of using inductive learning.

What follows is the "Assessment Target for Inductive Learning Examples: (Level 1) Inequalities, (Level 2) Topography, and (Level 3) Radioactive Dating."

Assessment Target for Inductive Learning Examples

Curriculum

Standard: from the district or state

Essential Question: (Level 1) What generalizations can we make about inequalities?
(Level 2) How can we draw mountains and valleys?
(Level 3) What generalizations can we make about radioactive dating?

Know: (Level 1) How to form generalizations about inequalities, inequality symbols; finding values for an unknown (i.e., x).
(Level 2) How to make predictions about key terms related to topography and contour map making.
(Level 3) How to form a generalization from information found through research, information about using radioactive dating processes, and how to draw conclusions and determine rationales for various types of dating.

Understand that: (Level 1) We can generalize information about inequalities by looking at examples of them.
(Level 2) We can make predictions about key words and phrases to discover how to use topography to make a contour map.
(Level 3) Radioactive or radiometric dating is a technique used to date materials, usually based on a comparison between the observed abundance of a naturally occurring radioactive isotope and its decay products, using known decay rates. Finding information about a topic can forms the basis for a generalization about it. (Retrieved June 2, 2009 from http://en.wikipedia.org/wiki/Radiometric_dating)

Do: (Level 1) Create generalizations about inequalities from examples of inequalities.
(Level 2) Create generalities about topography in order to make a contour map of a specified area.
(Level 3) Research a topic to form a generalization.

Measurable Objectives: (Level 1) 1. Students will compare, explain, generate, attribute, implement, differentiate, and produce a list of generalizations that are accurate about inequalities. 2. Students will compare, explain, generate, attribute, implement, differentiate, and produce a grouped list of inequality equations for each value of x
(Level 2) Students will compare, explain, generate, attribute, implement, differentiate, and produce a contour map that shows accurate and detailed information about the topography of a specific area.
(Level 3) Students will compare, explain, generate, attribute, implement, differentiate, and produce a list of generalizations that are accurate about radioactive dating.

Differentiation

Readiness: (Level 1) Teacher uses a whole-class process and graphic organizers.
(Level 2) Teacher-led process, using words that are not too challenging; graphic organizer helps students organize ideas for learning.
(Level 3) Teacher guides the process.

Interests: (Level 1) Students generate their own examples of the concept.
(Level 2) Students apply ideas to an art project.
(Level 3) Pictures that the teacher shows combined with investigation using computers pique students' interest in the topic.

Learning Styles: (Level 1) Self-expressive, analytical, mathematical/logical
(Level 2) Self-expressive, analytical, mathematical/logical, visual arts
(Level 3) Self-expressive, analytical, mathematical/logical, investigative

Procedures (Level 1)

♦ *Step 1:* Students brainstorm a list of things that are unequal. Record or ask a student to record students' answers. (DFA #1) Encourage students to find inequalities in the classroom, such as the following:

- Students of different heights.

- Hair cuts that are short and long.

- Pencils and pens that are different sizes.

Continue to list concrete ideas, but also prompt students to start thinking in terms of abstract numbers such as 3 < 4. Write the generated list and remind students about the inequality sign they learned about in elementary school. For students who struggle with abstract concepts, you may want to act out some inequalities and/or show pictures of them.

♦ *Step 2:* Give students several situations that require them to determine which numbers are less than, equal to, or greater than other numbers. Use informal formative assessments such as secret voting (having students close their eyes for voting or asking them to keep their vote private by putting their fists close to their chests) with thumbs up or thumbs down to determine who is understanding. Encourage students to make their own decision about the answers to your probes so that you can tell if they understand or not. Assure them that your primary concern is that they understand, and if they are dishonest about their answers, you cannot tell. (DFA #2)

♦ *Step 3:* Introduce the idea of inequalities in terms of an unknown value like x. Write the equation x < 5 and ask students to state what x might be. (DFA #3)

♦ *Step 4:* Ask students to generalize about the relationships between two unequal or equal values. Teachers hand out or ask students to draw a graphic organizer that captures the process of applying their generalizations, which are predictions of how equalities work. Figure 4.1 (page 76) is an example. (DFA #4)

Figure 4.1. Graphic Organizers for Testing Generalizations/Predictions

Generalization/Predictions	Evidence to Support	Evidence to Refute
There are certain rules we must follow to solve simple inequalities.	There are three basic rules: (list)	
We must flip the inequality sign when we multiply or divide by a negative value.	This is in rule 3.	
We can solve for an unknown using inequalities.	Many examples show how we can find values for inequalities.	
We can solve for two unknowns using inequalities.		I do not see any examples that prove this can happen.

- *Step 5:* Ask students to use their text book or other resources to provide support for their predictions or to refute them. (DFA # 5)

- *Step 6:* After introducing inequalities by the method above, another way to continue inductive learning with this topic is to present several types of simple inequalities that have the same answers. See the Level 1 "Measurable Objective" #2 for this part of the assessment, which states: "Students will compare, explain, generate, attribute, implement, differentiate, and produce a grouped list of inequality equations that are accurate for each value of x."

- *Step 7:* Ask students to examine and solve the equalities listed on the "Inequalities Sheet" (Figure 4.2). (DFA #6)

Figure 4.2. Inequalities Sheet

$-6x < -12$	$x + 5 < 7$	$2 + x > 4$	$-11x \geq -22$
$-x/2 < 1$	$-x + 7 \geq 5$	$x - 12 < -10$	$-8x < -16$
$x - 3 \geq -1$	$x/-2 > -1$	$x - 8 \leq -6$	$-x - 5 \leq -7$
$x/2 \leq 1$	$4 + x > 6$	$-6x > -12$	$-x + 7 \leq 5$
$11x \geq 22$			

- *Step 8:* Ask students to group the solutions using the "Inequalities Groupings Chart" shown in Figure 4.3. (DFA #6) Depending on the level of the class, the teacher may or may not fill in the labels across the top of the organizer.

Figure 4.3. Inequalities Groupings

x < 2	x ≤ 2	x > 2	x ≥ 2
$x+5 < 7$	$-x+7 \geq 5$	$x-3 > -1$	$-x+7 \leq 5$
$-6x > -12$	$x-8 \leq -6$	$2+x > 4$	$4+x \geq 6$
$-x/2 < 1$	$-11x \geq -22$	$x/-2 > -1$	$11x \geq 22$
$x-12 < -10$	$-x-5 \leq -7$	$-8x < -16$	$x/2 \geq 1$
$-6x > -12$			

Subsequent formative assessments and a final summative assessment could determine students' ability to solve problems applying their understanding of inequalities.

Procedures (Level 2)

♦ *Step 1:* Tell students that they are going to learn how to create a scientific picture of an area using knowledge of topography and contour map making. Explain that you will provide key terms that they should explore in their textbook (or an easier-to-read source) so that they will be able to accomplish this goal. There are several online resources that might help students learn about topography and contour map making. Here is one website that walks middle and high school students through the process of making a contour map: http://www.globe.gov/tctg/atla-contour.pdf?sectionId=28 (retrieved December 15, 2008).

♦ *Step 2:* Hand out the following list of ideas for students to group: elevation, landform, high relief, low relief, contour map, topography, plain, mountain, plateau, heights, sea level, feet, inches, lines, curves, hill, valley, ridge, distance, three-dimensional, two-dimensional, mountain range, smooth, flat, area, square miles, contour lines, scale, symbols, and color.

♦ *Step 3:* Hand out a graphic organizer (Figure 4.4) to help students keep track of their ideas. Show them an example of grouping and labeling the ideas on the list. For example: elevation, relief, and landforms can be labeled "topography." Remind students that words can go in more than one category. For Level 1 students, consider giving them the basic categories and asking them to add others.

Figure 4.4. Graphic Organizer for Grouping and Labeling

Topography	Measurement	Landforms
elevation, landforms, relief	inches, feet, square miles	mountain range, hill, plain, plateau, valley, mountain

Dimension	Map Making	Surfaces
two-dimensional, three-dimensional contour lines, distance	contour lines, scale, symbols, lines, curves, distance	flat, smooth, relief, color

- *Step 4:* Allow students to work with a partner or in a small group to group the ideas and label them. These groupings and labels are predictions at this point. (DFA #1)

- *Step 5:* As students read about making contour maps, ask them to find support for their ideas or information that would cause them to change their predictions. (DFA #2)

- *Step 6:* Show students examples of contour maps and help them use their new predictions to read them. (DFA #3)

- *Step 7:* Provide supplies so that students might make a simple contour map of a familiar area that has some elevation and some valleys. (DFA #4)

Summative assessment can include asking students to read a contour map or to answer specific questions about topography and contour map making.

Procedures (Level 3)

This assignment can be fun for teachers and students, if teachers find interesting pictures to "hook" their interest. Teachers can access wonderful pictures by going to Google Images and making slides using a PowerPoint program. These pictures serve the purpose of asking students to generalize about what they might mean. I have included a list of picture ideas and included a web address from which to find excellent pictures that teachers can copy. Make sure to credit these sources in your presentation and at the end make a "Fair Use Slide."

- *Step 1:* Choose a topic for students to explore, for example, "Radioactive Dating." Begin the session by showing several pictures. What follows is a list and description of several picture options (all retrieved December 15, 2008):

- A picture of an ancient scroll can be found at http://spencer.lib.ku.edu/sc/

- A picture of an ancient coin can be found at http://www-scf.usc.edu/~ciccone/images/greek%20silver%20coin.jpg

- A picture of a hieroglyph can be found at http://blog.bibleplaces.com/uploaded_images/Hieroglyphics_inscribed_on_rock_in_Wadi_Kharig,_tb032406542–706437.jpg

- A picture of interesting rock formations can be found at http://www.latimes.com/media/photo/2007-11/33907954.jpg

- A picture of a man on the moon can be found at http://starchild.gsfc.nasa.gov/Images/StarChild/space_level2/aldrin_big.gif

As students look at the pictures, have them make a list of ideas related to radioactive dating. They might talk about purposes for dating an item, what they know about radioactivity, and how dating might include math concepts like formulas and percentages. Record or ask a student to record students' answers. (DFA #1)

♦ *Step 2:* If computers are available, allow students to explore this topic online in order to find examples of radioactive dating. Students may also look at the information in their textbooks to add to their knowledge of this topic. Continue to list students' ideas and to clarify and answer their questions. (DFA #1 continues)

♦ *Step 3:* Give students several situations that might require radioactive dating and ask them to determine the best dating process—potassium-argon or carbon-14. Prompt students to also determine the percentage of radioactive element after a specified number of half-lives. (DFA #2)

♦ *Step 4:* Ask students to generalize about the uses and procedures involved in radioactive dating and to test their generalizations based on further exploration of the topic in the textbook or other sources. (DFA # 3) What follows are some possible generalizations or essential ideas students might conclude in terms of radioactive dating:

- Because geologists can learn the absolute ages of rocks using radioactive dating, we are better able to learn about the development of our planet.

- Scientists can use carbon-14 dating to determine the ages of materials made from plants or animals, because these materials are no older than 50,000 years.

- Scientists have used radioactive dating of moon rocks to tell us the age of the earth.

- We can determine the percentage of a radioactive element by multiplying one-half the number of years, setting up a proportion and cross-multiplying to solve for the unknown percentage.

- Knowing that half-life is the amount of time it takes for half of the radioactive atoms to decay helps us understand how radioactive dating works.

The students' abilities to generalize show that they have understood the information they have found in their textbooks or from other sources. The teacher might also assess students' ability to compute the ages of items based on the formulas. (DFA # 4)

Summative assessment can be a series of problems that require students to use various processes of radioactive dating.

Metaphorical Expression

This is a way of assessing students' ability to make meaning through a creative process of comparison. The example presented here combines mathematics and science topics.

Metaphorical Expression Example

- *Adjustment for struggling learners:* Before using this example with struggling learners, teachers should consider modeling the process with a simpler set of concepts and one with which students are familiar from their culture, for example, doing a math problem and making a meal. Teachers might also complete parts of the graphic organizer to prompt students' responses.

- *Adjustment for typical learners:* Typical learners should be able to enjoy this kind of assessment strategy; however, they may need some prompting to reach a level of creativity that makes this activity most interesting. Using whole-class interaction can make this higher-thinking process accessible to typical learners.

- *Adjustment for gifted or highly advanced learners:* These learners may enjoy a slightly more complicated process called "Synectics." See example on page 83.

What follows is the "Assessment Target for Metaphorical Expression: Waves and Algebra."

Assessment Target for Metaphorical Expression Example: Waves and Algebra

Curriculum
Standard: from the district or state
Essential Question: How are waves and algebra problems similar? How is a science phenomenon similar to an algebra problem?
Know: How to compare an algebra problem in terms of a science phenomenon.
Understand that: Comparing an algebra problem with how waves are formed helps us to better understand both processes.
Do: Use metaphorical expressions to compare math and science concepts. Create a new metaphor based on this process.
Measurable Objective: Students will generate, compare, create, and critique in order to produce metaphorical statement and creative products that expand and enhance understanding of how waves are formed and algebra problems solved.

Differentiation
Readiness: (Level 1) Use an easier comparison topic to prepare students to work with the example presented here; complete parts of the graphic organizer as prompts for students. (Level 2) Whole-class teacher modeling.
Interests: Students generate creative ideas.
Learning Styles: Self-expressive, analytical, creative, artistic

Procedures

- *Step 1:* Introduce the idea that students will use metaphorical expression to understand an algebra problem in terms of an ocean wave. Either direct students to the textbook or hand out an explanation about the graphic organizer (Figure 4.5).

- *Step 2:* Lead a whole class interactive discussion to help students determine how to apply information about making waves to the parts of a mathematics problem. Model this process for students by completing the first row of boxes of this graphic organizer. This is DFA #1. After you have demonstrated the process, ask students to complete each row of the organizer on their own or with a partner. To scaffold, assess each row students complete. (DFAs #2–5)

- *Step 3:* Allow students to work with a partner to complete another metaphorical expression based on your math or science unit of study. This creation is DFA #6.

Summative assessment can be a test, extended writing, or a project demonstrating knowledge of both ocean waves and algebra problems.

Figure 4.5. Metaphorical Comparison Chart on How a Wave is like Problem Solving

Step #	Making Waves	Math Problem	Steps to Problem Solving
1	Waves start in the open ocean and we do not know how large or strong they will be.	25 Surfers bought their boards at the surf shop. Some of the surfers spent $100 dollars for their boards and others that were lucky spent only $50. The surf shop owner made $1,500. How many surfers paid full price?	Read the problem and begin thinking about how to organize the data. When we first get a problem, we have unknown values. We do not know what the result will be, and in comparison, we do not know how large the wave will be.

Figure continues on next page.

2	The size of the wave varies depending on the amount of time and the strength of the winds that blow across the ocean	Let x = number of surfers who spent $100 Let $25-x$ = number of surfers who spent $50 Let $100x$ = the number of the surfers who spent $100 Let $50(25-x)$ = the number of surfers who spent $50	Convert the problem to unknown values. The amount of the variables depends on monetary values and total amounts. The amount of time and strength of winds represent the variables for making waves.
3	First the breezes transfer their energy to the water, next the wave (not the water) moves toward shore, as it nears shore, the wave height increases and wave length decreases.	$100x + 50(25-x) = 1,500$ $100x + 1250 - 50x = 1,500$ $50x + 1250 = 1,500$	Follow the order of operations. The problem follows a specific order, just as a wave develops in a specific manner.
4	Wave height is figured through a simple mathematical process of determining the difference between its trough and its crest.	$50x + 1250\ (-1250) = 1,500\ (-1250)$ $50x = 250$ $50x / 50 = 250/50$	Use simple operations, subtraction and division to solve for x. We also use simple operations to determine the height of a wave.
5	The wave is resolved when it reaches the shore.	$x = 5$ 5 surfers paid full price	Equation solved; wave crashes on shore

Source: This example is based on an example from Silver, Strong, and Perini, 2007, p. 135.

Synectics Example

Gifted or highly advanced learners can make great use of the synectics process, which comes from the work of Gordon (1961). This form of assessment evaluates students' ability to make meaning through a creative process of comparison.

What follows is the "Assessment Target for Synectics Example: Parabolas and Emotions."

Assessment Target for Synectics Example: Parabolas and Emotions

Curriculum
Standard: from the district or state
Essential Question: How are parabolas and emotions are similar?
Know: How to brainstorm connections between two unlike things to note metaphorical connections; create products that connect two unlike concepts; concepts of parabolas and feelings.
Understand that: We can compare parabolas and emotions to help us deepen our understanding and knowledge of each.
Do: Use the synectics process to deepen our understanding of parabolas and emotions.
Measurable Objective: Students will generate, compare, create, and critique metaphorical statements and creative products that expand and enhance their understanding of parabolas and emotions.

Differentiation
Readiness: (Level 3) Teacher guides students through a process.
Interests: Students brainstorm and draw from their own experiences and interests.
Learning Styles: Self-expressive, analytical, creative

Procedures

In each step, the teacher or designated student records the remarks of students as they brainstorm. The teacher makes it clear to students that no answer is silly or stupid and no one should criticize or make negative statements about any remark.

- ◆ *Step 1:* Ask students to work alone or with a partner in order to write their answers to this question: What is a parabola? Teacher records all answers students might give about parabolas. Answers could be as follows: a curve; the graph of a quadratic function; has symmetry; has a vertex at its highest or lowest point; when the vertex is the minimum or lowest part of the parabola it opens upward; when the vertex is the maximum or highest point the parabola opens downward. Elicit deeper conceptualizations by asking questions, such as when do we use parabolas? How do we graph them? You might draw some lines on graph paper that are or are not parabolas to help students practice identifying them. (DFA #1)

♦ *Step 2:* Ask students to create an analogy by writing the answer to this question: How is a parabola like an emotion? Answers can be as follows: both have shape; both are nonlinear; both have cause and effect; both have direction; both can show upward movement (a smile) and downward movement (a frown); both have symmetry in terms of opposites; both can be pointed or flat; both have functions that shape them. Ask students to visualize and feel how a parabola might be like an emotion: a sad parabola; a happy parabola; a parabola that shows pointed feelings; a parabola that shows blunted feelings; a parabola that shows opposite feelings; a quadratic function that creates a happy parabola; one that creates a pointed emotion; actions that, like functions, create emotion, such as an argument with a friend, which has many variables can create a downward emotional picture. (DFA #2)

♦ *Step 3:* Ask students to draw one of the analogies on a sheet of paper. For example, a parabola that shows opposites of emotion, a parabola that shows heightened emotions, a parabola that shows dulled emotions. Ask students to also write the quadratic function that creates the parabola and use pictures to illustrate the variables that create the emotional picture. (DFA #3)

♦ *Step 4:* Students explore as a whole-class discussion or with a partner how some of the words they have listed seem to be in conflict; for example, "pointed" and "flat" show conflicting emotions and conflicting quadratic functions; "direction," "cause and effect," and "nonlinear" show how a parabola and an emotion can have direction and show cause and effect, but can move in a nonlinear manner.

♦ *Step 5:* Facilitate students' finding a new analogy that might produce a creative product. For example, students could decide that the best new analogy compares nonlinear to lines and emotions that do not move in a straight direction. (DFA #4)

♦ *Step 6:* Look for words or phrases that "redefine" parabolas and that make learning about them a richer experience. For example, when we create parabolas from quadratic functions, we can see how they move in an upward or downward, pointed or flat direction, and we can associate that movement with our emotional lives. Also, when we think of our emotions we can think about how a quadratic function is like a series of events that create a parabola showing an upward or downward picture, just like our faces show upward or downward look on our faces. Finally, when we think of a graph as the context of our experiences, we can think of the parabola's location on that graph we might attach that location with an emotional state. Here are some suggestions for assessment products. Students' responses are DFA #5.

  • Graph the parabolas for four quadratic equations (supplied by the teacher or in the textbook). Write a short composition explaining how the parabolas are similar and different. Use "feeling" words to help you write your comparison paper.

  • Create pictures of the variables for at least four quadratic functions, show the parabolas they will create, and explain how these pictures are relevant to emotional states.

  • Write a report on how a quadratic function and its parabola might apply to a psychological or sociological issue.

  • Create a graphic organizer that analyzes in detail how parabolas and emotions are similar and different.

- Create a film about "The Parabola that Wouldn't Change."

Summative assessments can require students to show what they know about a unit that has explored quadratic equations and parabolas. It could require students to work problems in which they must graph parabolas based on equations.

Pattern Maker

This strategy, based on the work of Gick and Holyoak (1980) and also known as extrapolation, is a great tool for assessing students' mathematics or science learning. It provides a way to help learners see how noting patterns can help them create or problem solve. In this assessment, teachers provide one or more "analogues," which are the sources of the pattern or patterns, that help typical students solve new problems or create new products. Assessment includes determining how well the students accurately identify the structure of the analogue and how they apply that understanding to solve a problem or create a product.

Pattern Maker Example

- *Adjustment for struggling learners:* This strategy is a way to help struggling learners see how noting patterns can help them create or problem solve. For struggling learners, teachers must very clearly expose the patterns of the analogue as it applies to new problems. For this example, teachers may use three-dimensional analogues of plant and animal cells. They might also use a "tableau," which is a scene created by members of the class who are in appropriate costumes that represent animal and cell parts. These visual and kinesthetic aids will help struggling students see a clear picture of the parts of the cell.

- *Adjustment for typical learners:* These learners may be able to see the analogues through less time-consuming and concrete processes.

- *Adjustment for gifted or highly advanced learners:* Teachers might extend the procedures to include an enrichment activity based on students' learning. For example teachers might assign students to complete a creative project, such as a photo story, a short film, or a podcast, to show what they have learned about the parts of animal and plant cells through the pattern maker process.

What follows is the "Assessment Target for Pattern Maker Example: The Cell."

Assessment Target for Pattern Maker Example: The Cell

Curriculum
Standard: from the district or state
Essential Question: How can we best discover the parts of plant and animal cells?
Know: How to use an analogue of plant and animal cells to label real plant and animal cells; the parts of plant and animal cells.
Understand that: Looking at patterns in an analogue about plant and animal cells can help us create or discover those same patterns in real cells under a microscope.

Do: Use an analogue (picture of plant and animal cells) to label real plant and animal cells.

Measurable Objective: (Levels 1, 2, and 3) Students will generate, compare, and organize a description of patterns that help them to accurately label the parts of animal and plant cells they view under a microscope.
(Level 3) Students will generate, organize and create an original product that is accurate and sufficient about the parts of animal and plant cells.

Differentiation

Readiness: (Level 1) Teachers use visuals that are three-dimenstional and/or a kinesthetic activity as analogues for the assignment.
(Level 2) Teachers model the process for the whole class.
(Level 3) Students create a special product to demonstrate extension of learning.

Interests: Students allowed to use interesting equipment to investigate a real science topic.

Learning Styles: Self-expressive, investigative, analytical, visual

Procedures

♦ *Step 1:* Show several pictures of different kinds of cells. At this point, students only see physical features of these cells. They do not know the names of these features. Pictures could be hard copy or on a PowerPoint slide. Pictures could include all kinds of plant and animal cells. For struggling students, teachers can use three-dimensional analogues or a "tableau," as mentioned previously. Ask students to note any patterns they see in the pictures, three-dimensional analogue, or tableau. They might note lines, colors, textures, shapes, etc. (DFA #1)

♦ *Step 2:* If you use a picture, overlay labels that identify various parts of plant and animal cells. If you use three-dimensional models or a tableau, add labels at this point.

♦ *Step 3:* Ask students again to note patterns they see. Answers might include cell walls; cell membranes; organelles; nuclear envelope; chromatin; nucleolus; mitochondria; endoplasmic reticulum; ribosomes; Golgi bodies; chloroplasts; vacuoles; lysosomes; etc. (DFA #2)

♦ *Step 4:* Elicit a response that prompts students to compare and contrast animal and plant cells and to wonder how all the cell parts work within the cell. Use a chart like a Venn Diagram (see Figure 1.1, page 5, for an example) to show a comparison of plant and animal cells. (DFA #3)

♦ *Step 5:* Give students a picture of an unlabeled plant cell and an unlabeled animal cell. Using the analogue as a guide, help students practice labeling the parts of these cells. Teachers might also allow students to color these parts using a key (e.g., cell walls—red; cell membrane—green; organelles—purple). (DFA #4)

- *Step 6:* Ask students to look at a real plant cell and a real animal cell under a microscope, and ask them to label these real cells from the patterns they noticed in the pictures. Go online to find excellent pictures of plant and animal cells. You might google plant and animal cell images or use your textbook. (DFA #5)

- *Step 7:* Ask students to think about how they used the analogues presented to help them see the patterns necessary to label the real cells. (DFA #6)

Summative assessment could be a multiple-choice or short-answer test, extended writing, or a project about plant and animal cells.

Visualizing and Mind's Eye

This strategy, which comes from the work of Keene and Zimmerman (1997) and others, as adapted by Silver, Strong, and Perini (2007), can assess students' abilities to translate written or spoken words into pictures.

Mind's Eye Example

For this strategy teachers may use the same process with various topics based on students' readiness levels. The provided example is leveled for gifted or highly advanced students in terms of subject matter; however, I have suggested other topics for struggling and typical learners who can follow the same process.

- *Adjustment for struggling learners:* Use this same process with a geometry concept like circumference.

- *Adjustment for typical learners:* Use this same process with a geometry concept like plane geometry.

- *Adjustment for gifted or highly advanced learners:* This strategy works well for gifted or highly advanced learners because it allows them to explore an exciting new science idea—fractal geometry.

What follows is the "Assessment Target for Mind's Eye Example: Fractal Geometry."

Assessment Target for Mind's Eye: Fractal Geometry

Curriculum
Standard: from the district or state
Essential Question: (Level 1) What is circumference?   (Level 2) What is plane geometry?   (Level 3) What is fractal geometry?
Know: How to use drawing, questioning, predicting, and expressing a personal feeling to understand a mathematical concept.
Understand that: Using a visualizing process can help us better understand complex mathematical concepts.

Do: Follow a process of drawing, questioning, predicting, and expressing a personal feeling to understand a mathematics concept.

Measurable Objective: Students will exemplify and create a picture, a question, a prediction, or a personal feeling that demonstrates an accurate and thorough response about a mathematics concept.

Differentiation

Readiness: Levels 1, 2, and 3: Teacher facilitates the same process with different topics.

Interests: Choosing among drawing, questioning, predicting, and expressing a personal feeling are engaging processes.

Learning Styles: Self-expressive, visual, mathematical/logical, analytical, kinesthetic (drawing)

Procedures

♦ *Step 1:* Choose a group of sixteen to twenty words that represent a unit of study. For example you might teach a unit on fractal geometry. You can find excellent descriptions of this new science at http://classes.yale.edu/fractals/ (retrieved December 12, 2008).

Here are some terms: familiar symmetries; self-similarity; initiators; generators; geometry of plane transformations; inverse problems; random algorithm; fractals in architecture; self-infinity; Iterated Function System; statistical self similarity; fractal forgeries; mechanics of transformation; image compression; African repetition; Indian repetition; European repetition.

♦ *Step 2:* Read the words slowly, one at a time, and ask students to create a mental picture of them one at a time. For example, read the words *familiar symmetries* and ask students to imagine a familiar symmetry. Check to make sure each person has visualized these words. (DFA #1) As you continue reading the words, encourage students to adjust their imaginings of what the words might mean.

♦ *Step 3:* After you have read all the words, ask student to do one of the following four things. This is DFA #2.

• Draw a picture of your image.

• Write a question you hope the unit will answer.

• Create a prediction you think the unit will answer.

• Describe a personal feeling you have when you visualize the information.

♦ *Step 4:* Allow students to share their ideas with the class. (DFA #3)

- *Step 5:* Ask students to individually read about fractal geometry to check out how their work compares with the real information in the unit.

- *Step 6:* Have a class discussion about what students found. (DFA #4)

Next steps might include teaching students to collect words and to use the same process. Summative assessment might be asking students to apply their understanding of fractal geometry to one or more real-world problems.

Summary

This chapter presents examples in all three levels of self-expressive formative assessments; for example, inductive learning, metaphorical expression and Synectics, pattern making, visualizing, and mind's eye. Students who prefer self-expressive learning strategies enjoy using their imaginations and being creative. Notice that these strategies require high-level thinking skills and allow teachers to assess students often. Students can learn these processes and use them with a variety of topics.

5

Interpersonal-Based Differentiated Formative Assessments

This chapter provides leveled examples of embedding formative assessments into a specific differentiated instructional strategy called *interpersonal-based learning*. Interpersonal-based assessments use students' natural inclination to work together and to help each other. These kinds of assessments, with some teacher guidance and prompting, should inspire most students to learn; however, they especially appeal to students who feel a need to form a personal relationship with the learning activities and with their fellow students. These students want to feel of sense of belonging and their priority is relationship building.

Reciprocal Learning

According to Silver, Strong, and Perini (2007), many researchers have shown the benefits of students coaching each other. Students can learn more when they play the role of coach. This strategy offers many opportunities to use formative assessments of fact-based learning.

Reciprocal Learning Example

♦ *Adjustment for struggling learners:* This lesson is leveled for typical learners; teachers can adjust it for struggling learners by using material that is on the instructional reading level for the majority of the class. Teachers should also use additional modeling of the process and should identify and exclude any students who might be resistant to working as a coach for another student. Teachers might have a more structured lesson available for that possibility.

♦ *Adjustment for typical learners:* For this process, typical learners may need to have some advanced preparation. Teachers may choose to role play how one person might coach another one using an example from one of the assignment sheets.

♦ *Adjustment for gifted or highly advanced learners:* To structure this lesson for gifted or highly advanced students, teachers might use a more challenging text and might develop higher-level questions.

What follows is the "Assessment Target for Reciprocal Learning Example: Periodic Table."

Assessment Target for Reciprocal Learning Example: Periodic Table

Curriculum
Standard: from the district or state
Essential Question: What is important to remember about the Periodic Table?
Know: How to coach someone to review facts about the Periodic Table.
Understand that: Students can help each other through coaching to better remember facts about the Periodic Table.
Do: Coach a student through learning facts about the Periodic Table.
Measurable Objective: Students will recall and produce answers on an assignment sheet that reflects accurate information about the Periodic Table.

Differentiation
Readiness: (Level 1) Use material on instructional reading level of class. (Level 2) Teacher-guided process, modeling, and checking for readiness to proceed on their own. (Level 3) Use more challenging materials and more challenging questions.
Interests: Working with another student is interesting to most students.
Learning Styles: Interpersonal, investigative, visual and auditory

Procedures

♦ *Step 1:* Develop assignment sheets of review questions (Figure 5.1) on the Periodic Table. Create one assignment sheet for Partner A and one for Partner B. Partner A's assignment sheet should have hints and answers to Partner B's answer sheet and vice versa.

♦ *Step 2:* Assign partners or instruct students to select a partner who will work with them for the period. You might use the "point to your partner" technique explained in Chapter 2, page 32. Tell students that they should next decide who is partner A and who is partner B. Next tell students that they will take turns helping one another complete an assignment sheet as a way to review the Periodic Table.

♦ *Step 3:* Tell students that you are going to practice a process called *reciprocal learning*. Have a brief conversation with them about what it means to "coach" a fellow student and, if necessary, role play the process with a cooperative student. (DFA #1)

Figure 5.1. A and B Assignment Sheets: Periodic Table

Assignment A

5 B Boron 10.81	6 C Carbon 12.011	7 N Nitrogen 14.007
13 Al Aluminum 26.982	14 Si Silicon 28.086	15 P Phosphorus 30.974

Use the above area of the Periodic Chart to answer the following questions.

1. Which element has an atomic number that is closest to half of its atomic mass?
2. Which element has the heaviest atomic mass?
3. What atomic number comes before Boron and what atomic number comes after Phosphorus?
4. How many electrons are in Aluminum?
5. Aluminum is a _____ (metal, metalloid, or nonmetal).
6. Boron and Aluminum are in the same _____?

Assignment B

16 S Sulfur 32.06	17 Cl Chlorine 35.453	18 Ar Argon 39.948
34 Se Selenium 78.96	35 Br Bromine 79.904	36 Kr Krypton 83.80

Use the above area of the Periodic Chart to answer the following questions.

1. Sulfur, Chlorine, and Argon are in the same _____.
2. Which element's atom number exactly equals the atomic number of another element when doubled?
3. If Ar, Cl, and Kr are written in red that means they are _____ (solids, liquids, or gases).
4. All of these elements are in green boxes, which means they are all _____ (metal, metalloid, nonmetal).
5. Which two elements have the closest atomic masses?
6. Which element has the lightest atomic mass?

Key B & (Hints)

1. Period (Rows are called? Think about sentences.)
2. Argon (Look at the top numbers and double each top number; 18 × 2 = ?)
3. Gases (Think about the element you know most about—chlorine. You can smell it in a pool, but it's not liquid.)
4. Nonmetal (Do you recognize any of these elements? Are any of them metal? If they are all the same, use the process of elimination.)
5. Selenium and Bromine (Look at the bottom number. Which two numbers are most similar in value? If you cannot estimate, subtract.)
6. Sulfur (Look at the bottom number. Which whole number is the smallest?)

Key A & (Hints)

1. Nitrogen (Look at top number and bottom number. Which bottom number has the smallest remainder?)
2. Phosphorus (Look at the bottom number. Which whole number is largest?)
3. 4 comes before Boron and 16 comes after Phosphorus (Think about the whole chart and how the elements are arranged.)
4. 13 (Look at the top number. The top number is the number of protons. The number of protons is the same as what?)
5. Metal (Think about aluminum foil. Does it look like a metal?)
6. Family or group (Columns are called? Think about relatives.)

- *Step 4:* Hand out assignment sheets to partners A and B. Circulate and troubleshoot to make sure students are "coaching" each other appropriately. Partner A's sheet will include "Assignment A" and "Key B & (Hints)." Partner B's sheet will include "Assignment B" and "Key A & (Hints)." (DFA #2)

- *Step 5:* Evaluate the process with students. (DFA #3)

Summative assessments can include a multiple-choice or short-answer test, an extended writing assignment, or a project on the Periodic Table.

Problem Solving and Decision Making

Problem Solving Using a Decision-Making Model

- *Adjustment for struggling learners:* To adjust this lesson that is leveled for typical learners, teachers might work through the entire process as a whole-class activity rather than allowing students to get into groups. Teachers could also propose a few clearly structured problems and allow students to vote on the one they want to solve.

- *Adjustment for typical learners:* One of the best ways to get typical learners interested in learning is to find a problem that they care about solving. Typical learners often have problems connecting academic subjects such as math to real world problems. This assessment strategy is an interesting way to get typical learners personally involved in a topic, and it allows them to work with others, which is highly attractive to them. Teachers should choose a topic about which they know students are passionate or, as with the struggling learners, they might allow students to vote on that topic. (This is a preassessment.) They should plan to interest students in the problem by showing a PowerPoint presentation or reading an online or hard copy article in a journal, magazine, or newspaper. The lesson included here is a math example that provides a means for the teacher to assess typical students' learning math content as well as a decision-making process that might apply to other problems. In this example, the teacher presents the problem.

- *Adjustment for gifted or highly advanced learners:* To adjust this strategy for gifted or highly advanced teachers should require that students "find" their own problem or teachers might present a problem that is "fuzzy" because it includes unnecessary, confusing, or ambiguous information. Teachers or students might find these problems in the real world by reading online or hard copy journals, newspapers, or magazines. Except for finding the problem, the steps of the process are identical. Teachers and student groups should collaborate to determine the theme and essential questions during this process. Teachers can see Waterman (2006) for a template and examples of using a process called "Student-led Unit Planning," in which students decide themes and determine essential questions that their research might answer. In this situation, the students might choose the general science theme: the environment. For this fuzzy problem finding, use the step below and then use the steps presented in Figure 5.2, page 96.

- *Step 1:* Allow students to work with a partner or in a small group. Ask them to read an online or hard copy journal, newspaper story, or a magazine article about the environment with the purpose of finding a problem that they might use a decision-making process to solve. (DFA #1)

What follows are the "Assessment Target for Problem-Solving and Decision-Making Example: School Problem."

Assessment Target for Problem-Solving and Decision-Making Example: School Problem

Curriculum
Standard: from the district or state
Essential Question: (Levels 1 and 2) How might we raise money to solve a problem at our school? (Level 3) How might we find and solve a problem in our environment?
Know: How to make decisions that help us solve a problem.
Understand that: We can solve problems through a structured decision-making process.
Do: Use a structured decision making process to solve a real-world problem.
Measurable Objective: (Levels 1 and 2) Students will compare, implement, differentiate, critique, and produce data resulting from a decision-making process that leads to an efficient plan to solve the problem of raising money for school. (Level 3) Students will compare, implement, differentiate, critique, and produce data resulting from a decision-making process that leads to an efficient plan to solve a problem concerning the environment.
Differentiation
Readiness: (Level 1) Work through the process with the whole class rather than allowing students to get into small groups; choose a structured problem in which most students are interested, use the example presented here, find another, or allow students to vote on one from among those proposed by the teacher. (Level 2) Teacher-guided process, templates, and checkpoint assessments (Level 3) Use the same process but with a "fuzzy" or "found" problem about the environment; ask students to determine the criteria for evaluating solutions to the problem.
Interests: Working on a problem in which students are interested.
Learning Styles: Interpersonal, investigative, mathematical/logical, creativity

Procedures

♦ *Step 1:* Assuming that most typical learners are interested in earning money, put students in groups of four or five, and then present this challenge:

We want to raise money for our school. (The more specific the need for the money, the better. Teachers could make this problem even more meaningful if students could actually raise the money for a team, club, or class.) I am proposing a competition to see which group can raise the most money. Your challenge is to choose a money-raising project and to determine the exact amount you could make if all goes as planned.

Figure 5.2 provides the problem-solving and decision-making steps.

Figure 5.2. Problem-Solving and Decision-Making Steps

- *Step 1:* What are the problems and challenges associated with raising money? Answers could include: picking something for which people will pay, finding something that does not take too much money to produce, keeping good records, advertising. (DFA#1)

- *Step 2:* Each group decides which of the statements about challenges (or a combination of statements) if solved would do the most to solve the problem of raising money.

  Help the students construct a statement that includes a condition statement and a key verb phrase that explains what should happen and under what circumstances it should happen. Here is an example of this kind of statement. Our school needs money for _____. What project might we plan so that we can make the most money by the last month of school? (DFA #2)

- *Step 3:* Teachers charge each group with thinking of a list of five solutions to the problem. Consult with each team to make sure they have identified excellent solutions. (DFA #3)

  Solutions could be as follows (DFA #4):

  1. Find a company that provides products for students to sell.

  2. Have a school dance.

  3. Have a carnival.

  4. Have a bake sale.

  5. Have a cooperative garage sale.

- *Step 4:* Students choose criteria to evaluate each of the five solutions. Teacher checks criteria. (DFA #4) Criteria could be as follows:

  Criterion 1: On which solution might students spend the most money?

  Criterion 2: Which solution costs the least amount of money to produce?

  Criterion 3: Which solution takes the least amount of time to create?

  Criterion 4: Which solution would present the fewest roadblocks?

  Criterion 5: Which solution would be the most fun to do?

- *Step 5:* Use the following chart to evaluate each of the solutions for each of the criteria. Prior to filling out this criteria, students must "do the math" before answering which solution might make the most money. For instance, members of the group must fill out the template titled "Expenses and Profits" (Figure 5.4, page 98). Do C1 with each solution before moving on to C2 and so on. (DFA #5)

Solution	C1	C2	C3	C4	C5	Total
S#1: Selling company						
S#2: Dance						
S#3: Carnival						
S#4: Bake sale						
S#5: Garage sale						

For each solution, give each criterion a score from 1 to 5, with 1 being the lowest and 5 being the highest score. Add up the numbers and note the solution that gets the most points.

♦ *Step 6:* Students make a plan explaining how they might conduct their fundraising activity. They include in the plan who will do what; where and how they will get their information; and other specifics. Each group should write its own plan, and then share the plan with the class. Students may actually decide to carry out their plan, but it is not necessary. (DFA #6)

The blank template shown in Figure 5.3 will help students organize and record the process.

Figure 5.3. Blank Template to Organize and Record the Process

♦ *Step 1:* What are the problems and challenges associated with raising money?

♦ *Step 2:* Write the statement your group decides is the critical issue that if solved would make the most money.

♦ *Step 3:* Write the five solutions the group generates as follows:

1. _____

2. _____

3. _____

4. _____

5. _____

♦ *Step 4:* Choose criteria to evaluate each of the five solutions:

Criterion 1:

Criterion 2:

Criterion 3:

Criterion 4:

Criterion 5:

♦ *Step 5:* Use the following chart to evaluate each of the solutions for each of the criteria.

Figure continues on next page.

Solution	C1	C2	C3	C4	C5	Total
S#1:						
S#2:						
S#3:						
S#4:						
S#5:						

For each solution, give each criterion a score from 1 to 5, with 1 being the lowest and 5 being the highest score. Add up the numbers and note the solution that gets the most points. Do one criterion at a time and try not to give a score more than once.

◆ *Step 6:* Write a plan for conducting your fundraiser. Include how you would gather information, who would do what, and when they would do it. Share your plan with the class.

Expenses and Profits Template Suggestion

Students should create a format that matches their fundraiser best. Figure 5.4 is a generic template.

Figure 5.4. Fundraiser Template

Name of the Fundraiser: _____	
Projected Expenses (such as advertising, materials, time, supplies, equipment)	1. $_____ 2. $_____ 3. $_____ 4. $_____ *Add more as needed* *Total: $_____*
Projected Gross Income (such as what you will earn for each item you sell)	1. $_____ 2. $_____ 3. $_____ 4. $_____ *Add more as needed* *Total: $_____*
Projected Total Profit (which is Gross Income *minus* Expenses)	T. $_____

Summative assessments might include asking students to write about the process or evaluating their explanation of the problem solution.

Jigsaw

This is an excellent cooperative learning strategy that comes from the work of Aronson (1978). As cooperative learning, it is ideal for middle and high school students. Any information can be "jigsawed" by dividing it into reasonable segments. In addition, the jigsaw process involves having two groups: a home group and a study group. Learning occurs when students teach each other the "jigsawed" information. This section presents a strategy for struggling learners.

♦ *Adjustment for struggling learners:* It may be best to use the Jigsaw process to review information that students have already learned in more traditional ways. Example 1 is "Adding, Subtracting, Multiplying, and Dividing Fractions."

♦ *Adjustment for typical learners:* Teachers should use this activity as they explore "materials" such as polymers and composites, metals and alloys, ceramics and glass, and radioactive elements. The only difference between "Jigsaw" for typical learners and "Jigsaw" for struggling learners is that typical learners might learn new information through this method rather than using it as a review. Example 2 is "Materials."

♦ *Adjustment for gifted or advanced learners:* Use the same process for any unit of study. Make sure you have reading materials that are on students' advanced reading level. These students might explore "materials" using higher-level reading selections.

What follows is the "Assessment Target for Jigsaw Examples: Adding, Subtracting, Multiplying, and Dividing Fractions (Level 1); Materials (Levels 2 and 3)"

Assessment Target for Jigsaw Examples

Curriculum
Standard: from the district or state
Essential Question: (Level 1) What are the procedures for adding, subtracting, multiplying, and dividing fractions? (Levels 2 and 3) How do we use various materials such as polymers and composites, metals and alloys, ceramics and glass, and radioactive elements?
Know: (Level 1) How to add, subtract, multiply, and divide fractions; how to review these skills with peers. (Level s 2 and 3) How to teach others about various materials; information about various materials; how to work effectively in a group.
Understand that: (Level 1) Adding, subtracting, multiplying, and dividing fractions are important basic mathematical processes. (Levels 2 and 3) Materials such as polymers and composites, metals and alloys, ceramics and glass, and radioactive elements have important uses in our lives.
Do: (Level 1) Review how to add, subtract, multiply, and divide fractions. (Levels 2 and 3) Read about a determined type of material, plan how to teach the information to peers, teach the information, and assess the learning.

Assessment continues on next page.

Measurable Objective: (Level 1) Students will summarize, compare, explain, organize, differentiate, plan, and produce teaching materials that adequately and accurately review information about adding, subtracting, multiplying, and dividing fractions. (Levels 2 and 3) Students will summarize, compare, explain, organize, differentiate, plan, and produce teaching materials that adequately and accurately explore uses of the following materials: polymers and composites, metals and alloys, ceramics and glass, and radioactive elements.

Differentiation

Readiness: (Level 1) Use the process as review and use materials on students' instructional reading level.
(Level 2) Use the process to introduce new information on students' independent reading level.
(Level 3) Use the process to introduce new information using advanced materials.

Interests: Creating teaching materials and helping each other learn; working in a group to learn together; choosing how to teach a topic.

Learning Styles: Interpersonal, visual, creative, logical/mathematical, investigative, visual and auditory

Procedures (Level 1)

Teachers should use this activity as a review of fractions, not students' first experience with them.

♦ *Step 1:* Put each student in a home group. Tell students to number off, one to four. If you have to make any groups of more than four, let two students share responsibility for a topic.

♦ *Step 2:* Give the students who are number four a handout that describes how to add fractions; give students who are number three a handout that describes how to subtract fractions; give students who are number two a handout that describes how to multiply fractions; and give students who are number one a handout that describes how to divide fractions.

♦ *Step 3:* Teachers should designate a one table, a two table, a three table, and a four table, and instruct students to move to these tables based on their assigned numbers. Tell students at each table that they should read their handouts and complete some products to review with their home group about their topic. Structure this activity by giving students some cards and markers so that they can construct flashcards or other devices to help students review their topic. The materials they construct are DFA #1.

♦ *Step 4:* When students return to their home groups, they should take turns (starting with adding fractions) reviewing with their home group about their topic. (DFA #2)

♦ *Step 5:* Assess students on the "jigsawed" information and give extra credit to students whose reviewing seemed to have helped students do well on the teacher's assessment. (DFA #3)

Summative assessments include asking students to solve problems that require them to add, subtract, multiply, or divide fractions.

Procedures (Levels 2 and 3)

Teachers can use these procedures to introduce the topic of materials to typical and gifted or highly advanced learners. Typical learners might use textbook resources and gifted or highly advanced students might use resources from the Internet or other hard copy sources.

♦ *Step 1:* Put each student in a home group. Tell students to number off, one to four. If you have to make any groups of more than four, let two students share responsibility for a topic.

♦ *Step 2:* Use the textbook and ask students who are number four to read the section that describes polymers and composites; ask students who are number three to read the section that describes metals and alloys; ask students who are number two to read the section that describes ceramics and glass; and ask the students who are number one the read the section that describes radioactive elements.

♦ *Step 3:* Teachers should designate a one table, a two table, a three table, and a four table, and instruct students to move to these tables based on their assigned numbers. Tell students at each table that they should read their sections of the textbook and complete some products with which to teach their home group about their topic. For gifted or highly advanced students, teachers might assign each number group to investigate its topic on the Internet in order to develop ideas to present to their home group. Give students some cards and markers so that they might construct flashcards or other learning aids that teach about their topic. The materials they construct are DFA #1.

♦ *Step 4:* When students return to their home groups, they should take turns teaching about their designated topic. (DFA #2)

Summative assessments include asking students to take a multiple-choice or short-answer test, write a composition, or do a project based on what they have learned about materials.

Community Circle

This strategy, which according to Silver, Strong, and Perini (2007) is based on substantive research, is a way to allow students a chance to voice their thoughts, feelings, and values. It is not to be confused with a Socratic seminar, which assesses what students might have learned about a topic. This process is more like a classroom meeting during which the teacher might assess concerns students are having about an issue in class, or the teacher could use it to assess students' prior knowledge and understanding of a math or science topic. The process works best for most students if they are in a circle. Generic steps are as follows:

♦ *Step 1:* Determine a topic based on a unit you are studying.

♦ *Step 2:* Seat students in a circle.

- *Step 3:* Pose the topic and allow each student to make a comment, one by one, taking turns around the circle. The topic may go around the circle several times before it has been thoroughly discussed. (DFA #1)

- *Step 4:* After students have finished discussing the topic, the teacher asks them to reflect on what was said and to note patterns. (DFA #2)

- *Step 5:* Pose synthesis questions that ask students to continue to reflect on their participation in the circle and to draw conclusions about the topic. (DFA #3)

Teachers should move students toward taking leadership roles in this process. Teachers might use the Q-Space (Figure 5.5) to enhance the discussion.

Figure 5.5. Q-Space

For the Community Circle or to deepen any discussion the teacher might use a strategy called Q-Space (developed by Strong, Hanson, & Silver, 1998):

- Questioning (e.g., "Why do we need to know about science?")
- Silence and wait time (i.e., allow "thinking" time)
- Probing (e.g., "Can you tell us some more about that? Or why?")
- Accepting (e.g., "Thank you for sharing that idea." *Note:* Avoid saying "You are right!")
- Clarifying (e.g., "I am not sure what you mean. Can you clarify?")
- Correcting (e.g., "I do not think that idea has been proven. Could you rethink that?")
- Elaborating (e.g., "Could you say more about that?")

Sliver et al. (2007) also suggest that teachers might use a variety of question types to address various learning styles. They suggest teachers use the following types of questions for any of the appropriate Q-Space categories listed in Figure 5.5 (e.g., teachers might use a literal, analytical, creative, or personal question stem as the Questioning, Probing, or Elaborating):

- Literal (e.g., How is the Periodic Chart organized? What do we do when we have a negative variable and we're trying to solve an inequality?)
- Analytical (e.g., What evidence can you provide for your answer?)
- Creative (e.g., How can your imagination help you find a solution to…?)
- Personal (e.g., How does this situation make you feel?)

What follows are discussion topics for struggling learners, typical learners, and gifted or advanced learners. Within these topics, teachers might use the four kinds of questions to prompt student participation and Q-Space to deepen the discussion process. Teachers might also teach student how to write these kinds of questions and ask them to bring one question for each category to the community circle. Students seem to become more engaged in a discussion if they feel responsible for making it interesting through their own questions.

Math (Struggling Learners)

- Why do we need math (algebra, geometry)? (analytical)
- Is there such a condition as "math anxiety?" (literal)

- What would make you "fall in love" with math (algebra, geometry)? (personal)

- Why is it important to solve for an unknown quantity? (analytical)

- Math lovers versus math haters: a discussion of differences. (personal)

- What is the most important concept in math (algebra, geometry)? (personal)

- How would you use math skills to plan a recreational activity? (creative)

- How would you use math skills to solve a financial problem? (creative)

Science (Struggling Learners)

- Why do parents need to know about science? (analytical)

- If you became a scientist, what would you study? (personal)

- Science lovers versus science haters: a discussion of differences. (analytical)

- Why do we need science (biology, physics, chemistry)? (analytical)

- How does knowledge of science help me stay healthy? (analytical)

- How does knowledge of science make me a better citizen? (personal)

- What careers rely on a solid knowledge of science (biology, chemistry, physics)? (literal)

- If you could create a new science, what would it be? (creative)

Math (Typical Learners)

- What are the most important tools of math (algebra, geometry)? (literal)

- How is math (algebra, geometry) useful to you? (personal)

- Why is it important to follow the procedures established for solving math problems, such as the order of operations and the law of exponents? (analytical)

- Why is it important to use formulas to solve problems? (analytical)

- What are the most important uses of measurement? (analytical)

- How might your imagination help you learn to analyze mathematical data? (creative)

Science (Typical Learners)

- Why is it important to learn to formulate hypotheses? (analytical)

- Why is it critical to learn science laboratory safety rules? (analytical)

- What does it mean to feel like a scientist? (personal)

- How might the ability to analyze scientific data, have an impact on _____ (pick a topic such as medical discovery)? (analytical)

- Why is technology important to scientific discovery? (analytical)

- Why do scientists study the hydrosphere? (literal)

- How do you and your family affect the quality of our water? (personal)

- Why is it important to learn about the Periodic Table? (literal)

- How do chemicals affect human health conditions? (literal)

- How did the Earth evolve? (literal)

- How do maps and other technologies help us understand how the Earth has developed? (creative)

- How do cells keep all organisms alive? (literal)

- Why is it important to you to learn about microbiology? (personal)

Math (Gifted or Highly Advanced Learners)

- What is the most significant mathematical process and why? (literal)

- What would your life be without math? (personal)

- How does math make art better and vice versa? (creative)

- Why is it important to notice iterative and recursive patterns in math? (analytical)

- How is direct variation important for problem solving in the real world? (analytical)

Science (Gifted or Highly Advanced Learners)

- What is the most important scientific discovery? (literal)

- What do you think about global warming? (personal)

- What is a creative idea to deal with the oil shortage? (creative)

- What are the ethical issues involved in genetic engineering? (personal)

- What uses of biotechnology are the most important for the survival of our way of life? (analytical)

Summary

This chapter presents leveled examples of how to use interpersonal strategies to formatively assess student learning. These strategies address the needs of students who learn best when they feel a connection with others and with the topic. Teachers should enjoy using all of these different strategies within their units of study. The next chapter demonstrates how to include all four styles in the same unit to assess student learning.

6

Four Style Differentiated Formative Assessments

This chapter provides leveled examples of embedding formative assessments into all four learning styles—Mastery, Understanding, Interpersonal, and Self-Expressive—so as to help students balance them. It is important that students have experience with all four styles because students' learning styles are subject to change based on their interest in the topic and their readiness to learn it. These strategies also allow students to practice a variety of learning styles; I base these four style strategies on the work of Silver, Strong, and Perini (2007).

Window Notes

Window notes provide an alternative to traditional note taking. Using this method may motivate students to record information from a variety of learning styles. This method of note making asks students to focus on the facts and concepts embedded in the information (mastery), how they feel about that information (understanding), what questions they have about it (interpersonal), and what ideas or pictures come to their minds that they might draw to remember the topic (self-expressive).

- ◆ *Adjustment for struggling learners:* To adjust this strategy for struggling learners, teachers should use reading materials on students' instructional reading level. They should also use this strategy with the whole class for the first time, and they should preview the topic using concrete examples. They should also expect fewer and less detailed notes in the windows.

- ◆ *Adjustment for typical learners:* Teachers might introduce the lesson using a KWL strategy. After modeling the process with the whole class once or twice, teachers can expect these students to work on their own, with a partner, or in a small group. Teachers can expect students to record detailed responses.

- ◆ *Adjustment for gifted and highly advanced learners:* After brief modeling, teachers can expect these students to review independently; to complete the process independently, with a partner, or in a small group; and to record more detailed and higher-order thinking responses.

What follows is the "Assessment Target for Window Notes Example: Ratios and Rates."

Assessment Target for Window Notes Example: Ratios and Rates

Curriculum
Standard: from the district or state
Essential Question: What are the real-world applications for ratios and rates?
Know: Facts about ratios and rates; how to take window notes to help remember ideas about ratios and rates.
Understand that: Ratios and rates have real-world applications that are easy to remember by taking window notes.
Do: Make window notes to remember the concepts of ratios and rates.
Measurable Objective: Students will summarize, produce, exemplify, attribute, generate, and implement window notes that accurately and thoroughly note facts, feelings, questions, and pictures about ratios and rates.

Differentiation
Readiness: (Level 1) Teacher-led process and graphic organizer; use concrete examples to introduce the topic; expect fewer and less detailed notes. (Level 2) Teacher-led process and graphic organizer; use KWL to access prior knowledge; expect more detailed notes. (Level 3) Teacher-led process and graphic organizer; use independent review process; expect more detailed notes that show evidence of higher-order thinking.
Interests: Making abstract math concepts concrete and therefore more interesting.
Learning Styles: Interpersonal, mastery, self-expressive, understanding, visual

Procedures (General)

- *Step 1:* Announce to students that they will be taking notes from their text in a new way.

- *Step 2:* Hand out an 8 × 10 piece of white paper and model how to divide it into four equal boxes.

- *Step 3:* Ask students to label each box as shown in Figure 6.1.

Figure 6.1. Window Notes

Facts	Feelings
Questions	Ideas

Procedures (Level 1)

♦ *Step 4:* After completing Steps 1 to 3, explain the topic. For struggling learners, the best way to introduce the topic of ratios is to find a highly relevant and concrete example of a ratio. For example, if you want struggling learners to eventually understand that a ratio is the comparison of two numbers by division, depending on how well the students understand numbers and the process of division, you might begin with a concrete example by using manipulatives in which students make a ratio of one number of blocks to another, or you could ask student to act out a situation with a number of students on one side of the room and another number on the other side of the room. After students understand that a ratio is a comparison of one number to another, you should move on to Step 5. (DFA #1)

♦ *Step 5:* Instruct students to write the fact (definition) of ratio in the fact box and check to make sure that each student has written the correct definition. (DFA #2) Remind students that they will be getting more facts for this box, so that they will not fill the space with their writing.

♦ *Step 6:* Ask students to record how comfortable they are with this concept. For struggling learners, the teacher may need to help them identify some feelings including allowing them to rate their comfort level from 1 (being low) to 10 (being very comfortable) with their understanding of the concept. (DFA #3)

♦ *Step 7:* Allow students to write a question they might have. You can give students some ideas for possible questions, such as "Why would I use ratios in my life?" "How are ratios like fractions?" (DFA #4)

♦ *Step 8:* Ask students to draw a picture that might help them remember what a ratio is. (DFA #5)

♦ *Step 9:* Repeat this process with rate and unit rate, making sure to use concrete examples so that struggling learners might better understand these abstract concepts. For this Window Note, students should have three facts, three feelings, three questions, and three pictures. The teacher should collect this work to evaluate it, but return it to students so that they may keep it in a notebook for studying purposes. (DFA # 5)

Summative assessment can include asking students to work ratio and rates problems embedded in real-world events.

Procedures (Level 2)

♦ *Step 4:* After completing Steps 1 to 3, explain that the class will be learning about ratios and rates. For typical learners, the teacher might want students to go through the KWL process to access prior knowledge. (DFA #1)

♦ *Step 5:* Instruct students to read about ratios and rates in their textbook or another text. Ask them to collect facts, feelings, questions, and ideas in the correct boxes as they come to them. For this Window Note, students should find at least three detailed facts, feelings, questions, and ideas or pictures. Allow students to share one at a time from each of the four boxes. (DFA #2) Collect this work to evaluate it, but then return it to students so that they can keep it in a notebook for studying purposes.

Summative assessment can be a multiple-choice or short-answer test, an extended writing, or a project.

Procedures (Level 3)

♦ *Step 4:* After completing Steps 1 to 3, explain that students will be learning about ratios and rates. For gifted or highly advanced students, begin by asking student why learning about ratios and rates is important. (DFA #1)

♦ *Step 5:* Instruct the students to read about ratios and rates in a textbook or from an Internet resource. Ask them to complete the Window Notes (Figure 6.1, page 107). (DFA #2 to #5) Teachers might expect these students to write detailed information that shows evidence of higher order thinking skills.

Summative assessment can include asking students to use ratios on their own to solve complex word problems.

Circle of Knowledge/Seminar

This is a method of assessing students orally. Teachers should arrange the class in a circle and to avoid friends' talking to one another, they might assign seats in the circle. Most students are eager to share their thoughts and feelings, but shy students may need a teacher-facilitated chance to make a comment. Unlike the community discussions, this strategy allows the teacher to assess academic learning that is "tied to a text."

Circle of Knowledge/Seminar Example

♦ *Adjustment for struggling learners:* This lesson is leveled for typical learners. To adjust it for struggling learners, choose a text that the author has segmented with main ideas bolded and that may have some pictures as clues to the content. Also, teachers may want to make sure students have successfully written seminar questions. Teachers may want to collect the questions the day before the seminar and then hand them back to students as they get into the seminar circle. In this way, teachers can assure students through feedback (DFA #1) that their questions are useful for the discussion.

♦ *Adjustment for typical learners:* What follows is an example of a seminar experience for typical learners.

♦ *Adjustment for gifted or highly advanced learners:* To adjust this strategy for gifted or highly advanced learners, teachers should find a text that is both challenging and interesting to the majority of the class. Teachers might want to consider using a "Mini-Seminar—An Adaptation of Whole-Class Seminar" (page 112) with these students.

What follows is the "Assessment Target for Circle of Knowledge/Seminar Example: Famous Mathematicians."

Assessment Target for Circle of Knowledge/ Seminar Example: Famous Mathematicians

Curriculum
Standard: from the district or state
Essential Question: What can the lives of famous mathematicians teach us about the field of mathematics?
Know: How to share ideas with others by referencing the text; talking without relying on the teacher to call on them; making claims and supporting them; and not monopolizing the discussion.
Understand that: The lives of famous mathematicians can teach us important historical, social, and cultural information.
Do: Follow the rules for seminar discussion; write and answer challenging questions that are tied to a text about famous mathematicians; use appropriate social skills.
Measurable Objective: Students will explain, summarize, produce, exemplify, attribute, and generate oral responses that are respectful of others, are thorough and accurate, and that reference the text about the lives of famous mathematicians.

Differentiation
Readiness: (Level 1) Choose a reading selection that is on students' instructional reading level. (Level 2) Teacher-guided process with grade-level reading selection. (Level 3) Use the same process but with a more challenging text; consider a mini-seminar process.
Interests: Group discussion is motivating. Students enjoy sharing their opinions and ideas.
Learning Styles: Interpersonal, self-expressive, mastery, and understanding, verbal/linguistic, auditory

Procedures

♦ *Step 1:* Identify a grade-level and interesting text for the students to read on the topic of "Famous Mathematicians." This text could be in students' textbooks or one taken from another source such as the Internet. Ask students to read this selection and annotate it as best they can (annotation is making notes on the side with questions and other ideas). Their annotations could include responses to a specific theme or question. For example, ask students to note places in the text that show how the lives of famous mathematicians teach us about important historical, social, and cultural information.

♦ *Step 2:* Tell students that during the next class, they will be participating in a seminar discussion of this text and that everyone should bring at least two questions to help with the discussion. Teach students to write Level 2- and Level 3-type questions.

How to Write Seminar Questions

♦ *Step 3:* Explain to students that for seminar you will use the concept of three levels of questions (Costa & Kallick, 2000) and that because a Level 1 question has one answer, it is not an appropriate "discussion" question. Model how to construct a Level 2 question (one that the person answering must infer and that may have many answers) based on the text they have just read.

Here are some Level 2 examples for this topic:

• Which mathematician is most interesting to you?

• Which mathematician made the most important contribution to the world?

• Which mathematician's accomplishment impressed you the most?

• What kinds of patterns have you noticed in the ways mathematicians live their lives?

Walk around the room and have mini desk conferences to make sure each student knows how to write this kind of question. (DFA #1)

♦ *Step 4:* Show students how to write a Level 3 question that uses the text as a base, but moves beyond it into themes. For typical learners, provide this stem to get them started on this question level: "What does this text (*specify the title of the selection*) teach us about _____? (Model for them how they might supply a theme idea such as justice, responsibility, or violence.)

Here are some Level 3 examples:

• What do the lives of famous mathematicians teach us about following our dreams?

• Why are mathematicians important to the betterment of our world?

• How does the work of mathematicians affect teenagers?

• What do the lives of famous mathematicians teach us about the importance of math (algebra, geometry)?

Walk around to check that each student has successfully written a Level 3 question. (DFA #2)

♦ *Step 5:* Tell students that their "Ticket to seminar is two discussion questions about the text." Make sure each student has written these two questions before they leave class; you might even collect them so that they will be available for the next class. (DFA #3)

♦ *Step 6:* For the next class, arrange the desks in a circle.

♦ *Step 7:* As a member of the circle, explain the rules and expectations that you have also posted in the room for students to see. Another idea is to hand out a copy of the rules and expectations to students in addition to the posting of them. Figure 6.2 provides sample seminar rules and expectations.

Figure 6.2. Seminar Rules and Expectations

1. Be respectful of everyone.

2. You do not need to raise your hand to speak.

3. Keep your eyes on the person who is speaking.

4. Group conversations only.

5. Reference the text.

6. Use Standard English.

For each of these rules and expectations, stop and ask students to explain why this rule is important and model what it would look like as it is experienced. As the seminar proceeds, gently remind students to follow the correct procedures. Here are some good phrases to use:

♦ "Standard English, please."

♦ "You don't have to raise your hand, just speak out."

♦ "Can you reference the text?"

♦ "Help us find the words you are reading."

♦ *Step 8:* Begin the seminar by asking a question or asking a student to ask his or her question. Continue discussing the topic, famous mathematicians, until time is running out and the students have discussed most of the questions. Noting students' responses on a "Class Participation Grid" (Figure 6.3, page 112) is DFA #4.

♦ *Step 9:* To finish seminar, you may want to give shy or reluctant students a chance to speak. You may give these students a "parting shot" question that is relatively easy to answer.

Figure 6.3. Class Participation Grid

Student														Grade

To grade a seminar, the teacher may use the oral assessment grading grid. The grading grid (Figure 6.3) provides a chance to formatively assess students' orally.

List all the students in the class. Put a + or P for every positive comment the student makes in a class discussion and put a – for every negative behavior or comment the student makes during class discussion. Decide how many +s or Ps constitute an A, B, C, D, or F. Make sure to deduct minuses from the total pluses or checks.

Mini-Seminar: An Adaptation of Whole-Class Seminar

To offer a chance for even more intense conversation about a topic, teachers may want to divide the class in half, into medium-sized groups, or into groups of four or five. (*Note:* Only use this method after students have practiced the whole-class method of seminar discussion.) To use this adapted version of seminar, teachers should take the following steps:

- *Step 1:* Choose the content and a method of developing questions for the seminar. Supply the questions or require students to generate them.

- *Step 2:* Decide how to group the students. Here are some suggestions:

  - Divide the class in half. Have one group of quiet and perhaps shy students and another group of more outgoing and verbal students.

  - Divide the class based on learning styles.

  - Form heterogeneous groups of four or five, making sure each group has a strong student leader and a good mix of abilities.

- *Step 3:* Make sure each group has a leader and a recorder. The students can elect these leaders or the teacher can appoint them.

- *Step 4:* Give the instructions outlined in Figure 6.4.

- *Step 5:* Circulate constantly to assure that the discussions are going smoothly. Encourage groups to give each student a chance to talk. (DFA #1) Most gifted or highly advanced students take this process seriously and participate well.

Figure 6.4. Mini-Seminar Instructions

1. The group leader will keep the discussion going. He or she will ask questions and allow others to ask them.

2. The recorder should write on a sheet of paper the names of each member of the group leaving three or four spaces between the names. The recorder's job is to put a slash mark (/) each time a student makes a comment. It is the recorder's responsibility to make sure all students get credit for contributing to the conversation.

3. I will grade each of you on the number of comments you make that add to the conversation.

◆ *Step 6:* Evaluate the assessment by counting the number of comments each student makes in comparison with other members of the group. For example, some groups have students who make detailed remarks, and for these students their recorder may have recorded fewer comments. Teachers should determine the style of the group and adjust the grading to match it. (DFA #2)

Summative assessment can include asking students to write an extended response about the topic.

Do You Hear What I Hear? (DYHWIH)

This research-based strategy comes from the work of Strong, Silver, Perini, and Tuculescu (2002). The idea is that if students interact with a text several times and learn to retell it accurately, they will strengthen their comprehension skills. Teachers should consider using this strategy as a differentiated formative assessment at least once per week for three weeks and then on the fourth week, ask students to choose their best work for grading. This strategy uses partner and group work to motivate student engagement in text.

DYHWIH Example

These examples are based on the idea that teachers can differentiate a process by using different materials based on students' interests. According to Silver, Strong, and Perini (2007), teachers can find excellent sources of high-interest math problems online. They suggest the following websites: www.nctm.org (you have to join to get the problems), www.fi.edu/school (I liked this one best), and www2.edc.org/mathproblems. What follows is a suggestion for using the same process with three different problem ideas.

◆ *Adjustment for struggling learners:* This is a perfect strategy for struggling learners and often just what they need to improve their reading comprehension skills. I think that many struggling learners would be interested in the health of babies.

◆ *Adjustment for typical learners:* Typical learners should be able to use this strategy, which addresses all four learning styles, to improve their ability to solve real-world or rigorous math problems. I think a problem about caring for elephants will be interesting to typical learners.

◆ *Adjustment for gifted or highly advanced learners:* Gifted or highly advanced learners should be interested in a more complex set of problems, like rate of change.

What follows is the "Assessment Target for DYHWIH Example: Baby's Blood Type (Level 1), Taking Care of Elephants (Level 2), and Rate of Change (Level 3)."

Assessment Target for DYHWIH Examples

Curriculum
Standard: from the district or state
Essential Question: (Level 1) How do babies inherit their blood type? (Level 2) How can we use multiple mathematical steps to solve a problem about taking care of elephants? (Level 3) How can a rate of change formula help us organize important data into a useful graph?
Know: (Level 1) How to listen to a selection, take notes, retell, and write about the selection on a baby's blood type. (Level 2) How to listen to a math–science problem, make a picture of the problem, plan a solution to the problem, and solve it using multiplication, division, addition, and comparison with large numbers. (Level 3) How to solve a science–math problem by collecting data over time in order to use a rate of change formula that creates a graph; how to draw conclusions about collected data.
Understand that: (Level 1) Knowing facts about blood types can help avoid serious consequences. (Level 2) We can use multiple mathematical processes to solve a real-world problem about taking care of elephants. (Level 3) A rate of change formula can help organize important data into a useful graph.
Do: (Level 1) Listen to a selection about baby's blood type, take notes about it, retell and discuss questions about the selection. (Level 2) Listen to a math–science problem about caring for elephants, draw a picture of the problem; make a plan to solve it; solve it with a group. This is a multistep math problem. (Level 3) Solve a math–science problem by collecting data to use in a rate of change formula shown on a graph; draw conclusions about collected data.
Measurable Objective: (Level 1) Students will recall, generate, infer, organize, and create notes, oral responses, and a writing product that are accurate, sufficient, have technical quality, and are creative responses about a baby's blood type. (Level 2) Students will recall, generate, infer, organize, and create picture notes, oral responses, and a written solution that is accurate and detailed about caring for elephants. (Level 3) Students will interpret, apply, create, and generate to produce a response to a problem that demonstrates a thorough and accurate solution using applications of the rate of change formula.

Differentiation
Readiness: (Levels 1 abd 2) Teacher models the process and allows students to practice.
Interests: (Levels 1, 2, and 3) Using an interesting topic, addressing several learning styles, and allowing choice of writing product. (Level 3) Choice of problems to solve.
Learning Styles: Mastery, understanding, interpersonal, self-expression, verbal/linguistic, spatial

Procedures (Level 1)

♦ *Step 1:* Choose a relatively short (i.e., one or two pages), but relatively difficult selection that your students might find interesting and that addresses your curriculum. Write two to four guiding questions to use during Step 5 of the process. These questions might address the following categories: an important vocabulary term; an important quotation from the text; a question about the technique the author used to write the selection; and a question about the author's motivation for writing it.

To find an interesting and appropriately rigorous selection for struggling learners, you may need to go online instead of relying on your textbook. If you go online, print a class set of the selection. Here is the web address for an interesting selection on "Baby's Blood Type": http://www.keepkidshealthy.com/Newborn/babys_blood_type.html (retrieved December 18, 2008).

♦ *Step 2:* Tell students that you are going to read the selection to them twice. Once so that they can get the gist of it and a second time so that they can take notes or draw notes so that they can retell it to their partner. (DFA #1)

♦ *Step 3:* Read the selection to students for the gist. Read it again and check to make sure students are making notes the second time. This process addresses the self-expressive learning style. (DFA #2)

♦ *Step 4:* Either assign partners or allow students to choose a partner. Ask partner A to retell the selection without using his/her notes. Instruct Partner B to use his/her notes to coach partner A through the process to fine-tune the details. Then reverse roles and do the same. This process addresses interpersonal learning. (DFA #3)

♦ *Step 5:* Hand out or post guiding questions based on the selection. Figure 6.5 provides an example based on the article "Baby's Blood Type." Also, hand out a copy of the selection and ask students to read it silently. Ask students who complete the reading before others to begin thinking and perhaps writing answers to the four questions you posed.

Figure 6.5. Questions for "Baby's Blood Type"

Vocabulary: What does the author of this selection mean by the word *alleles*? (mastery)

Quotation: What does this quote imply? "With newer DNA testing, using blood types to determine paternity, or who the father is, isn't really that useful anymore." (understanding)

Technique: How does the fact that the writer addresses you in the first person affect your interest in the selection? (self-expressive)

Motivation: What do you think this writer wants you to learn from this selection? (interpersonal)

♦ *Step 6:* After everyone appears to have completed the reading, ask partners to join with other partners so that they form a group of four. Ask these groups to discuss the four questions and reach some kind of consensus on the answers. The four questions address all four learning styles: mastery, understanding, self-expressive, and interpersonal. (DFA# 4)

Note: For this step, you may need to establish a time limit, as well as model and practice the discussion process. Two options for helping students improve discussion skills are *Accountable Talk*, below, and *Q-Space* (see Figure 5.5, page 102).

Accountable Talk

Teachers might improve oral assessments if they use a strategy cited in Fisher and Frey (2007) called *Accountable Talk*, which was developed by Lauren Resnick (2000). It includes a list of agreements teachers and students make concerning student-to-student conversations. Accountable Talk includes the following three requirements that students learn, practice, and agree to maintain:

1. Staying on topic.

2. Using information that is accurate and appropriate.

3. Listening carefully and thinking about what others say.

Accountable talk also requires students to follow these strategies that they learn, practice, and maintain for each non–teacher-led discussion:

1. Press the speaker to clarify and explain. "Could you describe what you mean?"

2. Require the speaker to justify proposals or challenges to others' proposals by referencing the source. "Where did you find that information?"

3. Challenge ideas that seem wrong "I don't agree because…."

4. Ask the speaker to provide evidence for claims. "Can you give me an example?"

5. Use each other's statements. "Susan suggested… and I agree with her."

From Waterman (2009).

♦ *Step 7:* After students have discussed the four questions, assign a piece of writing that reflects their understanding of the selection. This writing should be one to one and one-half pages long and could be one of the following types of writing:

- Retelling

- Review
- Essay
- Creative response (i.e., a narrative or poem)
- Personal response

If you use this method three times during the month, you may want to ask for three different writing products. You may allow students to choose which of the three they use. You may also want to focus on one type of writing per month if you use this strategy throughout the year. Either provide a rubric for each kind of writing or use the generic rubric shown in Figure 6.6. (DFA #4)

Figure 6.6. Generic DYHWIH Rubric for Writing Products

Category	Level 1	Level 2	Level 3	Level 4
Accuracy	Has many inaccuracies that greatly distort the meaning of the selection.	At times the information appears inaccurate or questionable.	All information presented in the writing product is accurate and complete.	Presents accurate information and reasonable inferences and conclusions based on the selection.
Sufficiency	Lacks completeness and does not present a sufficient understanding of the selection.	Includes some details that show an understanding of the ideas of the selection, but they are not complete.	Details presented demonstrate understanding of the most important ideas from the selection.	Includes relevant and significant details that capture both the gist and thematic message of the selection.
Technical Quality	Significant loss of organization and focus and so many conventions errors that the piece is extremely hard to understand.	Shows some loss of control of organization and focus. Some conventions errors make understanding a problem for the audience.	Organized with few lapses in focus, and has no more than three conventions errors.	Well-organized, has minor to no evidence of conventions errors, and is closely focused on presenting the content and message of the selection.
Originality/ Style	Evidence of copying from the selection and no synthesis of information.	Does not include ideas that show new ideas generated by the selection.	Represents a personal synthesis of the selection.	Creative and demonstrates a clever perspective on the topic.

- *Step 8:* On the fourth week of using this process, allow students to review their writing and select one to share with a peer or in small groups. Silver, Strong, and Perini (2007) suggest that a "writing club" is a good idea to use for this step. (DFA # 5)

♦ *Step 9:* Students revise their work and submit for grading. This is a summative assessment.

Procedures (Level 2)

♦ *Step 1:* Select a problem. I have selected one about caring for elephants in India that integrates math and science. I found it at http://www.fi.edu/school/math3/elephants.html.

♦ *Step 2:* Tell students that you are going to read a math–science problem to them twice; once so that they can get the gist of it and a second time so that they can draw a picture that represents the problem. Tell them that they can use numbers and sketches, but no words.

♦ *Step 3:* Read the selection to students for its gist. Read it again and check to make sure students are making a sketch. This process addresses the self-expressive learning style. (DFA #1)

♦ *Step 4:* Give each student a copy of the problem, and make sure they do not solve it yet. Place them in small groups of three of four and ask them to do the following: show each other their sketches; work together to determine a clear definition of the problem; and make a plan for solving the problem. This process addresses interpersonal learning style. (DFA #2)

♦ *Step 5:* Walk around to note how students are working together to solve the problem. Ask one or two of the groups to share how they plan to solve it. This step includes mastery and understanding learning styles. (DFA #3)

♦ *Step 6:* Assign students to write a paper explaining how they solved the problem and a justification for why they solved it the way they did. (DFA #4)

♦ *Step 8:* In the fourth week of using this process, allow students to review the problems they have solved and select one to share with a peer or in small groups. (DFA # 5) *Note:* A way to make this problem more challenging is to require students to find out prices for elephant food and water.

♦ *Step 9:* Students revise their work and submit for grading. This is a summative assessment.

Procedures (Level 3)

Use the same process as above, but with a different problem. Figure 6.7 provides information regarding finding a math–science problem.

Summative assessment could be a multiple-choice test, a short-answer test, or one of the "Seven Types of Presentation Assessments" (see Chapter 1, page 16).

Figure 6.7. Finding a Math–Science Problem

Find a problem in science that requires the following:

♦ Collection of data over time

♦ Use of the rate of change formula and graphing.

Requirements:

♦ Collect data from your problem/experiment.

♦ Create a rate of change graph on a poster or in a PowerPoint presentation.

♦ Explain your findings in writing and orally in a presentation.

Holistic Project Standards

Level 1 (D)	Level 2 (C)	Level 3 (B)	Level 4 (A)
Data is inaccurate in places. Science topic is elementary and mostly common knowledge. Visuals are sloppy, disorganized, and insufficient.	Data includes some minor inaccuracies. Science topic is on grade level, but coverage is minimal. Visuals are organized and neat, but do not have a sense of originality.	Data is accurate. Science topic is on grade level and includes sufficient details. Visuals are organized and neat. The project is original and creative.	Data is accurate and extensive. Science topic is above grade level. It is highly complex and detailed. The project is organized, neat, highly original, and creative. It has an overall effect of Wow!

Task Rotation

This strategy incorporates the view that most students have one of the four learning styles: mastery, understanding, self-expressive or interpersonal. To use this strategy, teachers write tasks for each of these styles and decide if they want students to do one of the following:

♦ Complete all four tasks in a certain order.

♦ Complete all four tasks in the order students choose.

♦ Complete one or more tasks students choose and one the teacher chooses.

♦ Complete only one task that students choose.

Noting students' choices helps teachers to better understand their students' learning needs. I find this four-style concept of learning styles more useful than those that use visual, auditory, and kinesthetic and/or tactual learning because limiting the differentiation to sensory preferences also limits the variety of learning activities. I also find the four-learning style method more useful than using the seven multiple intelligences (Gardner, 1993) because of the sheer number of different assignments I have to write if I use it.

Task Rotation Example

For the task rotation example, I show how teachers might use different tasks based on students' readiness to address the same essential question and measurable objective. Teachers might help students determine their salient learning style using a checklist, such as that shown in Figure 6.8, prior to participating in task rotation. Teachers should inform students that they may have more than one style and that their style preference may change based on the task or content, and that they should practice using *all* styles.

 ♦ *Step 1:* Present the checklist (Figure 6.8) to students. Ask them to put a check by each statement that best matches their learning style. The box with the most checks indicates a preference. Teachers may use this information to help students choose tasks; however, they should keep in mind that students may shift their preference depending on the topic and the task.

Figure 6.8. Choose Your Style Checklist

Mastery Style	Interpersonal Style
I learn best by ☐ Seeing concrete evidence ☐ Practicing ☐ Knowing what to expect ☐ Finding "right answers" ☐ Doing drills and assignment sheets ☐ Knowing exact expectations ☐ Getting quick and accurate feedback ☐ Being recognized for work well done ☐ Being an active learner ☐ Having "hands-on" opportunities ☐ Seeing what to do (teacher modeling) ☐ Getting directions step by step I am able to organize _____	I learn best by ☐ Seeing how concepts relate to people ☐ Working with groups ☐ Sharing ideas ☐ Getting positive personal attention ☐ Role playing ☐ Learning about myself, especially feeling I am able to empathize _____
Understanding Style	**Self-Expressive Style**
I learn best by ☐ Analyzing situations ☐ Debating or arguing about ideas ☐ Working with other understanding-style students ☐ Thinking and studying the relationship among ideas ☐ Carrying out interesting projects ☐ Solving problems that require inquiry and evaluation I am able to interpret _____	I learn best by ☐ Multitasking ☐ Being creative ☐ Working with others on creative ideas ☐ Discussing open-ended questions and topics ☐ Discovering for myself ☐ Thinking outside the box ☐ Organizing in my own way I am able to create _____

Source: This chart is adapted from Silver, Strong, and Perini (as cited in Northey, 2005, p. 15).

 ♦ *Step 2:* After teachers have helped students determine their style preference, they should be ready to participate in a task rotation strategy.

- *Adjustment for struggling learners:* Allow these students to complete any of the task rotations; however, give them the opportunity to choose the less demanding tasks designed for them.

- *Adjustment for typical learners:* Instead of prescribing the sequence in which students should accomplish the tasks, teachers might allow students to choose the one they want to complete.

- *Adjustment for gifted or highly advanced learners:* Teachers might assume that these students can handle more rigorous academic demands as reflected in their task rotation assignments.

What follows is the "Assessment Target for Task Rotation Example: Stardust Elements."

Assessment Target for Task Rotation Example: Stardust Elements

Curriculum
Standard: from the district or state
Essential Question: How does studying the stars help us learn about our earth?
Know: Facts about stardust elements, including the processes of nuclear fusion, plasma, and supernova.
Understand that: Learning about elements from stardust helps us better understand elements on earth.
Do: At least one of the task rotation assignments.
Measurable Objective: Students will recall, generate, analyze, differentiate, and create in order to produce one (or more) task from the task rotation assignments that is accurate and detailed about stardust elements.

Differentiation
Readiness: (Level 1) Use Level 1 task rotation assignments. (Level 2) Use Level 2 task rotation assignments. (Level 3) Use Level 3 task rotation assignments.
Interests: Addresses several interesting options for learning.
Learning Styles: Mastery, understanding, interpersonal, self-expressive, mathematical/logical, spatial, visual, auditory, musical

Procedures

- *Step 1:* Develop the "Assessment Target," "Hook," and a "Task Rotation" (Figures 6.9, 6.10, and 6.11, all on page 122) for each of the three learner levels. Decide how to assign the tasks. For this assignment, it might be best to allow students to choose one task.

Figure 6.9. Level 1 Task Rotation: Stardust Elements

Mastery Task	Interpersonal Task
Make a quiz that has ten short-answer questions about stardust elements. Include an answer key.	Create a short (five slides at least) PowerPoint presentation about stardust elements.
Understanding Task	**Self-Expressive Task**
Write and present a one-minute speech on stardust elements.	Create a visual art product, write a song, or choose another form of art (with teacher approval) to show your understanding of stardust elements. Be prepared to tell the class about your work.

Figure 6.10. Level 2 Task Rotation: Stardust Elements

Mastery Task	Interpersonal Task
Make a board game with twenty short-answer mastery-based questions as a review about stardust elements.	Develop a short (eight slides at least) PowerPoint presentation for the class about stardust elements. You may work with a partner or in a group of three.
Understanding Task	**Self-Expressive Task**
Write a one-page report explaining the relationship between the Periodic Table and a supernova. Be sure to cite your sources.	Create a two- or three-dimensional visual art product, a dance, or a song that addresses topics in the unit. Suggestions include showing the process of nuclear fusion or a supernova. Products may be any kind of art and must include a paragraph of commentary, but get teacher approval first.

Figure 6.11. Level 3 Task Rotation: Stardust Elements

Mastery Task	Interpersonal Task
Design a creative game show based on the theme of stardust elements. Write a set of at least twenty short-answer questions for the show.	Create a PowerPoint presentation, a short film, a photo story, or a podcast based on your understanding of stardust elements.
Understanding Task	**Self-Expressive Task**
Complete a two-page research report with at least two sources of information that you cite on a "Works Cited" page on stardust elements.	Create an artistic product that clearly shows your understanding of stardust elements. Write a commentary explaining how the art answers the essential question about stardust elements.

- *Step 2:* Hook students' interest in this topic by showing a short film you can access from http://video.google.com/videosearch?q=supernova&emb=0&aq=f# (retrieved December 19, 2008). This is a 30-second film of the explosion of a supernova. It is interesting and a great hook for this lesson. Ask students to express their ideas about what they saw. (DFA #1)

- *Step 3:* Present information about stardust elements, including information about plasma, nuclear fusion, and supernovas. Present this information as a brief lecture, ask students to read about it in their textbooks, or provide online information that you might jigsaw. Most of the learning should come from students' participation in a task and their presentations to each other.

- *Step 4:* Tell students that they should choose from among the four tasks. Provide an evaluation tool for each task such as that shown in Figure 6.12. (DFA #2)

Figure 6.12. Evaluation Tools for Task Rotation: Stardust Elements

Tasks	Criteria
Mastery	See Figure 6.13. Mastery-Based Question Checklist and Figure 6.14. Mastery-Based Product Guide (page 124)
Interpersonal	See Figure 6.15. PowerPoint Speech Rubric (page 124)
Understanding	See Figure 6.16. Research Paper Holistic Rubric (page 126)
Self-Expressive	See Figure 6.17. Self-Expressive Product Guide (page 127)

Figure 6.13. Mastery-Based Question Checklist

Check off these criteria for the short-answer questions you will use for your mastery-based task.

General Criteria

____ Questions assess the essential knowledge and skills for this topic.

____ Questions do not require students to read at a level that might prevent them from showing what they actually know and understand.

____ Questions have no typos or mistakes that would confuse students.

____ Questions are culturally relevant and unbiased.

____ Questions are challenging, but not too hard for most students.

____ Directions for answering the questions are clear and easy to understand.

Short-Answer Criteria

____ Answers include a word or phrase.

____ Questions do not give clues to the answer (such as an, a).

____ Questions are in student-friendly language.

Source: The idea of a checklist comes from Linn and Miller as cited in Fisher and Frey (2007). I have adapted their adaptation of Linn and Miller. Teachers may need to meet with the students who have chosen this task to help them understand these criteria.

Figure 6.14. Mastery Product Guide

Product	Attributes
Quiz	The title of the quiz should be prominent, legible, and on topic. The directions for taking the quiz are clearly stated. Questions align with "Mastery-Based Question Checklist." All elements of the topic are covered. An answer "key" is provided. Answers are accurate.
Board Game	The title of the game should be prominent, legible, theme-based, concise, creative, original, and neat. The objective of the game is clearly stated within the directions. The directions and rules are clear, sequenced, neatly printed, and include the criteria for winning. The game board is clearly labeled in bold print. The board is poster-board size and is illustrated creatively. Game pieces are durable and a manageable size. All information is accurate. *(Adapted from Northey, 2005.)*
Game Show	The game show format is original and cleverly reflects the topic. The objective of the game is clearly stated within the directions. The rules of the game are clear and easy to follow. Questions align with "Mastery-Based Question Checklist." Students enjoy playing the game. All information is accurate.

Figure 6.15. PowerPoint Speech Rubric

	No Points	Loss of Substantial Points	Loss of Some Points	Maximum Points
Plan	Plan is incomplete.	Plan is not complete, but includes few of the assigned elements.	Plan is somewhat complete, and includes many assigned elements.	Plan is complete. Includes all assigned elements.
Organization of Content	No logical sequence of information.	Some logical sequence of information.	Logical sequence of information.	Logical and intuitive sequence of information.
Originality	The work is a minimal collection or rehash of other people's ideas and images. There is no evidence of new thought.	The work is mostly a collection of other people's ideas and images. There is little evidence of new thought or inventiveness.	The product shows some creative synthesis of research. Even though it is based on a collection of other people's ideas, the words and images go beyond that collection to offer some new insights.	The product shows significant evidence of creative synthesis of research. It demonstrates many new insights based on a depth of understanding that is based on logical conclusions and sound research.

	No Points	Loss of Substantial Points	Loss of Some Points	Maximum Points
Subject Knowledge	Subject knowledge is not evident. Information is confusing, incorrect, or flawed.	Some subject knowledge is evident. Some information is confusing, incorrect, or flawed.	Subject knowledge is evident in much of the product. Information is clear, appropriate, and correct.	Subject knowledge is evident throughout (more than required). All information is clear, appropriate, and correct.
Graphic Design	Graphics and/or pictures greatly interfere with the message.	Graphics and pictures seem random and at times out of balance. There is little sense of harmony and attractiveness. Sometimes the design competes with the message rather than supporting it.	Graphics and pictures combine with text to effectively deliver a strong message. Design techniques mostly work well together.	The combination of graphics, pictures, and text is superior and develops communication that exceeds any message that may have been presented without that combination. This creative combination connects elegantly with the intended audience.
Conventions	Presentation has four or more spelling errors and/or grammar errors.	Presentation has three misspellings or grammar errors.	Presentation has fewer than two misspellings and/or grammar errors.	Presentation has no misspellings and/or grammar errors.
Number and Type of Sources	No sources noted.	Sources are noted but are not in the correct form.	Four sources are noted but are not the correct types.	Four or more sources are noted in the correct form and the correct types.
Oral Presentation	Speaker does not stick to time limit. Speech is often inaudible. There is a negative or sarcastic attitude.	Speaker does not stick to time limit. Speech is inaudible. Speaker too often says "umm." There is a lack of conviction.	Speaker sticks to time limit (is only off slightly) and speaks distinctly and audibly with conviction.	Speaker sticks closely to time limit and speaks distinctly and audibly with conviction. Develops a charismatic relationship with audience.

Figure 6.16. Research Paper Holistic Rubric

1 (loss of more than 30 points)	2 (loss of 16–30 points)	3 (loss of between 1 and 15 points)	4 (no loss of points)
◆ Paper loses focus on the stated topic. ◆ Information is generally incomplete and inaccurate. ◆ Writer does not cite sources and may even plagiarize information. ◆ Information is disorganized and includes mostly common knowledge, quotes, or the writer's opinion. ◆ Ideas are not coherent or unified. ◆ Conventions errors make the paper difficult to read.	◆ The writer loses the focus on the topic one or more times. ◆ Information lacks a sense of completeness and is often inaccurate. ◆ Writer does not use the correct method for citing sources in the body of the paper. ◆ Information is not well-organized and is often common knowledge, a string of quotes, or the writer's opinion. ◆ Writers' ideas are not generally coherent or unified. ◆ Conventions errors make understanding the writing difficult.	◆ The writer consistently focuses on the stated topic. ◆ Information is complete and accurate. ◆ Writer sometimes does not use the correct method for citing sources in the body of the paper. ◆ Paper presents well-organized information that is most often beyond common knowledge or the writer's opinion. ◆ Writer presents ideas in a coherent and unified way. ◆ The writer has no more than six conventions errors.	◆ The writer focuses on the stated topic and makes it interesting for the audience. ◆ The writer presents information that is complete and accurately stated using the correct method for citing sources in the body of the paper. ◆ Paper presents well-organized information that extends beyond common knowledge or the writer's opinion. ◆ Writer presents ideas in a coherent and unified way. ◆ The writer has no more than three minor conventions errors.

Figure 6.17. Self-Expressive Art Product Guide

Product	Attributes
Visual Arts—Two-dimensional or three-dimensional picture	Addresses the task in an aesthetically pleasing and complete way by using abstraction, symbolism, and structure to show themes and relationships among key concepts within the topic. Includes a thorough and accurate commentary explaining the following: why you chose this artistic method to address the task; how the art shows themes and relationships within the topic; and how the product shows evidence of learning about the topic. It has a meaningful title.
Visual Arts—Poster	The title is prominent, concise, legible, in bold print, and describes the topic. Illustrations that address the key elements of the task are neat, colorful, and thorough. The text is legible, grammatically correct, and matches the purpose of the task. The poster appears to be balanced, uncluttered, compact, and uniform.
Performing Arts—Dance	Performance includes appropriate accompaniment and meaningful use of choreography to convey meaning associated with the topic; it is aesthetically pleasing and shows a high level of abstraction. The commentary must clearly explain the purposes of the movements as they are related to the topic.
Performing Arts—Original song or score	Song or score must address the key elements of the topic and include meaningful use of lyrics and/or melody to convey high levels of abstraction. Performance must have appropriate volume and clarity and be aesthetically pleasing. Commentary must explain how the song or score reflects key elements of the topic.

Source: Adapted from Northey (2005).

Summative assessments may include a short-answer test, extended writing, or another presentation of the material.

Summary

This chapter explains and exemplifies various readiness levels to show how to use four styles of differentiated formative assessments. Although teachers may use other forms of differentiated strategies to help them determine whether or not students are learning math and science facts and concepts, I chose to focus on these strategies from Silver, Strong, and Perini (2007) because they provide excellent variety and the capacity to sample deepening learning.

It is important to keep in mind that formative assessment should occur often and that, as much as possible, it should be differentiated to engage all kinds of learners. The most compelling purpose for differentiating formative assessment, however, is that it may help students stretch toward *higher readiness, new interests,* and a *variety of learning styles.* Differentiation is not about keeping students where they are as learners; it is about forever expanding their capabilities in a fair and respectful manner.

References

Ainsworth, L., & Viegut, D. (2006). *Common formative assessments: How to connect standards-based instruction and assessment.* Thousand Oaks, CA: Corwin Press.

Allen, D. (1998). The tuning protocol: Opening up reflection. In D. Allen (Ed.), *Assessing student learning: From grading to understanding* (pp. 87–104). New York, NY: Teachers College Press.

Allen, R. (2007). *TrainSmart: Effective training every time.* Thousand Oaks, CA: Corwin Press.

Anderson, L., Krathwohl, D., Airasian, P., Cruikshank, K, Mayer, R., Pintrich, P., Raths, J., & Wittrock, M. (Eds.). (2001). *A taxonomy for learning, teaching, and assessing: A revision of Bloom's taxonomy of educational objectives.* New York, NY: Longman.

Aronson, E. (1978). *The jigsaw classroom.* Beverly Hills, CA: Sage.

Ausubel, D. (1963). *The psychology of meaningful verbal learning.* New York, NY: Grune & Stratton.

Bangert-Drowns, R., Kulik, C., Kulik, J., & Morgan, M. (1991). The instructional effect of feedback in test-like events. *Review of Educational Research, 61*(2), 213–238.

Bloom, B. (1976). *Human characteristics and school learning.* New York, NY: McGraw Hill.

Blosser, P. (1973). *Handbook of effective questioning techniques.* Worthington, OH: Education Associations.

Blythe, T., Allen, D., & Powell, B. (1999). *Looking together at student work.* New York, NY: Teachers College Press.

Bruner, J. (1973). *Beyond the information given: Studies in the psychology of knowing.* Oxford, UK: W.W. Norton.

Buehl, D. (2009). *Classroom strategies for interactive learning.* Newark, DE: International Reading Association.

Buzan, T. (2000). *The mind map book.* New York, NY: Penguin Books.

Cain, M. (2005). *Mathability: Math in the real world.* Austin, TX: Prufrock Press.

Costa, A., & Kallick, B. (2000) *Habits of mind: Discovering and exploring.* Alexandria, VA: Association for Supervision and Curriculum Development.

DeVries, D., Edwards, K., & Slavin, R. (1978). Biracial learning teams and race relations in the classroom: Four field experiments using teams-games-tournaments. *Journal of Educational Psychology, 70*(3), 356–362.

Dunn, R. & Dunn, K. (1993). *Teaching secondary students through their individual learning styles: Practical approaches for grades 7–12.* Boston, MA: Allyn and Bacon.

Enright, B., Mannhardt, L., & Baker, L. (2004). *Algebraic thinking (part one)* (3rd ed.). Greensboro, NC: National Training Network.

Fisher, D., & Frey, N. (2007). *Checking for understanding: Formative assessment techniques for your classroom.* Alexandria, VA: Association for Supervision and Curriculum Development.

Frayer, D., Frederick, W., & Klausmeir, H. (1969). *A schema for testing the level of concept mastery.* Madison, WI: Wisconsin Center for Education Research.

Fulwiler, T. (1980). Journals across the disciplines. *The English Journal, 69*(9), 14–19.

Gardner, H. (1993). *Multiple intelligences: The theory in practice.* New York, NY: Basic Books.

Gick, M., & Holyoack, K. (1980). Analogical problem solving. *Cognitive Psychology, 12*, 306–355.

Gordon, W. (1961). *Synectics: The development of creative capacity*. New York, NY: Harper.

Guskey, T. (2007). Formative classroom and Benjamin S. Bloom: Theory, research, and practices. In J. McMillan (Ed.), *Formative classroom assessment: Theory into practice* (pp. 63–78). New York, NY: Teachers College Press.

Herber, H. (1970). *Teaching reading in the content area*. Englewood Cliffs, NJ: Prentice Hall.

Herman, J., Aschbacher, P., & Winters, L. (1992). *A practical guide to alternative assessment*. Alexandria, VA: Association for Supervision and Curriculum Development.

Hunter, R. (2004). *Madeline Hunter's mastery teaching: Increasing instructional effectiveness in elementary and secondary schools* (updated edition). Thousand Oaks, CA: Corwin Press.

Jung, C. (1923). *Psychological types* (H. G. Baynes, Trans.). New York, NY: Harcourt, Brace & Co.

Keene, E., & Zimmerman, S. (1997). *Mosaic of thought: Teaching comprehension in a reader's workshop*. Portsmouth, NH: Heinemann.

Kluger, A., & DeNisi, A. (1996). The effects of feedback interventions on performance: A historical review, a meta-analysis, and a preliminary feedback intervention theory. *Psychological Bulletin, 119*(2), 254–284.

Lyman, F. (1981). The responsive classroom discussion: The inclusion of all students. In A. Anderson (Ed.), *Mainstreaming digest* (pp. 109–113). College Park, MA: University of Maryland Press.

Marzano, R., Pickering, D., & Pollock, J. (2001). *Classroom instruction that works*. Alexandria, VA: Association for Supervision and Curriculum Development.

McDonald, J. (1996). *Redesigning school: Lessons for the 21st century*. San Francisco, CA: Jossey-Bass.

McDonald, J., Mohr, N., Dichter, A., Mcdonald, E. (2007). *The power of protocols: An educator's guide to better practices* (2nd ed.). New York, NY: Teachers College Press.

McMillan, J. (2007). Formative classroom assessment: The key to improving student achievement. In J. McMillan (Ed.), *Formative classroom assessment: Theory into practice* (pp. 1–7). New York, NY: Teachers College Press.

Milgram, R., Dunn, R., & Price, G. (Eds.). (2009). *Teaching and counseling gifted and talented adolescents*. Charlotte, NC: Information Age Publishing.

Mosston, M. (1972). *Teaching: From command to discovery*. Belmont, CA: Wadsworth Publishing.

Northey, S. (2005). *Handbook on Differentiating Instruction in Middle and High School*. Larchmont, NY: Eye On Education.

Ogle, D. (1986). K-W-L: A teaching model that develops active reading of expository text. *The Reading Teachers, 39*(6), 564–670.

Popham, W. (2008). *Transformative assessment*. Alexandria, VA: Association for Supervision and Curriculum Development.

Ramaprasad, A. (1983). On the definition of feedback. *Behavioral Science, 28*(1), 4–13.

Resnick, L. (2000). Making America smarter. *Education Week, 18*(40), 38–40.

Reynolds, S., Martin, K., & Groulx, J. (1995). Patterns of understanding. *Educational Assessment, 3*(4), 363–371.

Ross, M., & Mitchell, S. (1993). Assessing achievement in the arts. *British Journal of Aesthetics, 33*(2), 99–112.

Sagor, R., & Cox, J. (2004). *At-risk students: Reaching and teaching them* (2nd ed.). Larchmont, NY: Eye On Education.

Seidel, S., Walters, J., Kirby, E., Olff, N., Powell, K., Scripp, L., & Veenema, S. (1996). *Portfolio practices: Thinking through the assessment of student work.* Washington, DC: NEA Publication Library.

Silver, H., Strong, W., & Perini, M. (2007). *The strategic teacher: Selecting the right research-based strategy for every lesson.* Alexandria, VA: Association for Supervision and Curriculum Development.

Solomon, E., Berg, L., & Martin, D. (1998). *Thinking toward solutions: Problem based learning activities for general biology.* Florence, KY: Brooks Cole.

Stiggins, R., Arter, J., Chappuis, J., & Chappuis, S. (2007). *Classroom assessment* for *student learning: Doing it right—using it well.* Upper Saddle River, NJ: Merrill/Prentice Hall.

Strong, R., Hanson, J., & Silver, H. (1995). *Questioning styles and strategies* (3rd ed.). Woodbridge, NJ: Thoughtful Education Press.

Strong, R., Silver, H., Perini, M., & Tuculescu, G. (2002). *Reading for academic success: Powerful strategies for struggling, average, and advanced readers grades 7–12.* Thousand Oaks, CA: Corwin Press.

Suchman, J. (1966). *Developing inquiry.* Chicago, IL: Science Research Associates.

Taba, H. (1962). *Curriculum development, theory and practice.* New York, NY: Harcourt Brace & World.

Tyler, K., & Tyler, M. (2003). *Extreme math: Real math, real people, real sports.* Austin, TX: Prufrock Press.

Tyler, M. (2005). *Real life math mysteries: The kids answer to the question "what will we ever use this for?"* Austin, TX: Prufrock Press.

Vygotsky, L. (1986). *Thought and language.* Cambridge, MA: The MIT Press.

Waterman, S. (2006). *The democratic differentiated classroom.* Larchmont, NY: Eye On Education.

Waterman, S. (2009). *Differentiating assessment in middle and high school mathematics and science.* Larchmont, NY: Eye On Education

Wilhelm, J. (2001). *Improving comprehension with think-aloud strategies.* New York, NY: Scholastic Professional Books.

Wilhelm, J., Baker, T., & Dube, J. (2001). *Strategic reading: Guiding students to lifelong literacy, 6–12.* Portsmouth, NH: Heinemann.

Wiliam, D., & Leahy, S. (2007). A theoretical foundation for formative assessment. In J. McMillan (Ed.), *Formative classroom assessment: Theory into practice* (pp. 29–42). New York, NY: Teachers College Press.

Wormeli, R. (2006). *Fair isn't always equal; Assessing & grading in the differentiated classroom.* Portland, ME: Stenhouse Publishers.

Zaccaro, E., & Zaccaro, L. (2007). *25 Real life math investigations that will astound teachers and students.* Bellevue, IA: Hickory Grove Press.